Personal Finance
on the Net

Personal Finance on the Net

*Use the power of the Internet
to grow your personal wealth*

JOHN WHITELEY

How To Books

By the same author in this series:
Be Your Own Boss
Coping with Self Assessment
Managing Your Money in Retirement
Paying Less Tax

Published by How To Books Ltd,
3 Newtec Place, Magdalen Road,
Oxford OX4 1RE. United Kingdom.
Tel: (01865) 793806. Fax: (01865) 248780.
email: info@howtobooks.co.uk
http://www.howtobooks.co.uk

British Library Cataloguing in Publication Data.
A catalogue record for this book is available from
the British Library.

Edited by Julie Nelson
Cover design by Shireen Nathoo Design
Cover image by PhotoDisc
Cover copy by Sallyann Sheridan

Produced for How To Books by Deer Park Productions
Typeset by PDQ Typesetting, Newcastle-under-Lyme, Staffs.
Printed and bound by Cromwell Press, Trowbridge, Wiltshire

NOTE: The material contained in this book is set out in good
faith for general guidance and no liability can be accepted
for loss or expense incurred as a result of relying in particular
circumstances on statements made in the book. Laws and
regulations are complex and liable to change, and readers should
check the current position with the relevant authorities before
making personal arrangements.

Contents

List of Illustrations

1

Introduction

Handling your finances on the Internet does not have to be daunting or intimidating. If you have a good grasp of what is involved in your finances, and know your way round the Internet, then everything should fall into place. The business of handling your finances on the Internet, therefore, can be broken down into two parts:

- handling your finances
- using the Internet.

HANDLING YOUR FINANCES

Defining your objectives

The most important thing about dealing with your finances is to have an objective. The next most important thing is to have a plan to attain that objective. Nobody can tell you what your objectives are – or even what they should be. You may take advice, but in the end, you are the only person who can decide your own objectives. Of course, if you have a partner, you cannot take these decisions in isolation, and you should look at your objectives as a couple, or as a family. If you are undertaking this sort of exercise together, let all the family have the opportunity to put their ideas, and each member of the family should agree on the final product – at least for the time period which is relevant to them. For instance, a 16-year-old, who knows he is going to university in a couple of years' time, should have less say in the decisions about anything longer term than two or three years.

Therefore, the first step to taking control of your financial destiny is to sit down, think, and write down your financial objective. Do it now – don't read another word of this book until you have!

In fact, you may well find that you have more than one objective. If so, try to rank them in order of priority. You may well also find that you have different objectives for different time periods. You may have immediate objectives, medium-term objectives (say, for the next three years) and long-term objectives. In whatever form they come, you have now taken the first step towards taking contol.

Making your plans

Once you have defined your objectives, you must try to make plans so that you can achieve those objectives. For instance, you may have, as an objective, to get your spending under control, especially on non-essentials which all too often tempt you into impulse buying. To achieve that objective, you may decide to give yourself a budget of a set amount each week or month for pocket money. You can have that to spend as you wish, but once it is gone you have to wait until next week or next month.

Do you recognise that scenario? It is the sort of thing you may have been used to as children, with pocket money. It is still a good and valid way of applying self-discipline to your financial affairs as adults.

Monitoring your plans

Having made your plans, they are not much use unless you can see if they are working or not. Therefore take time to monitor your finances regularly. There are computer programs available to help you do this. The two market leaders are Microsoft Money and Quicken. These allow you to enter budgeted figures and compare them with your actual figures. Some web sites, particularly those dealing with online banking, allow you to download the details of your transactions directly into your Microsoft Money or Quicken programs.

Reviewing your plans

As we progress through life, our priorities change and we may need to change our financial objectives and plans. Take time, therefore, to review your objectives every few years and to change your plans accordingly.

USING THE INTERNET

There are many guides available to help you get started on the Internet. Why not start with *Using the Internet* by Graham Jones, published by How To Books?

The basics

All you need is a computer equipped with a modem, and a telephone line. You will have to make your own choice of Internet service provider. More providers are now providing a 'free' service. Some financial companies – banks, for example – also provide a free Internet service if you use their financial services.

Finding your way round

You will quickly realise that the World Wide Web is used by companies as a gigantic advertising hoarding. Their web sites may have all manner of interesting information, pictures, even games. But their main purpose is to get your business. The web actually does more than simply provide an advertising hoarding – it allows you to interact with the companies whose web sites you visit. This means you can sign up for their products, and even pay for the goods or services online.

Once you realise this aspect, you need not be overawed by it. The sheer volume of information allows you to make informed choices. If you are making a big decision or spending a lot of money, it may well pay to spend some time researching what is available.

This book aims to point you in the right direction – once you start exploring the Internet you will doubtless find other information for yourself.

Finding the addresses

Most of the references in this book are to web sites. The convention for addresses is to use lower case letters, and no spaces. The full address might read something like: http://www.moneyweb.co.uk. In these cases, I have omitted the 'http://' part of the address, beginning with 'www.'. In fact, if you type in the address starting with 'www.', in the address bar on your screen, the 'http://' part will be filled in for you.

In some cases, however, the pages are not part of the World Wide Web, and do not have a 'www.' address. In this case, I give the full address, including the 'http://' part. For instance, the address of Riley's is http://freespace.virgin.net/rileysinsurance.

Where I have listed sites dealing with particular subjects, I have mostly given some information about the sites. However, there are some sites that I have simply listed without any further information. That does not mean that they are not worth looking at. They will have some information about the subject which is useful.

Using search engines

If you are looking for information on the Internet, you may not know the address of the web site you are looking for. In fact, you may not even know what web site you need to go to. Search engines can help you to find the right place on the web. Your Internet Service Provider will give you access to a selection of search engines. Some of the biggest search engines are:

- Yahoo!
- AltaVista
- HotBot
- Excite
- Lycos

To find a subject with a search engine, simply type in the word or words you are looking for, and the search engine will find all the web sites on its register which refer to that word or subject. However, the World Wide Web is so vast that the search could come back with hundreds of thousands of results. While this may sound impressive, it would clearly be far too many for you to look at.

You can refine your search – for example, by asking for web sites in the UK only, or by asking for sites in a certain subject group. You can also refine the search by using more than one word, and asking the search engine to look for a group of words as a phrase. For instance, you could search for information on insurance. This would throw up many thousands of web sites. If, however, you refined your search to look for 'critical illness insurance' as a phrase, you would then narrow down the search, and get the web sites that are more relevant to you.

Printing out

If you want to print out the page you have been viewing, it is quite easy – just the press of a button. However, you will find that some web sites have dark backgrounds, with the text in white or a different colour. There may also be a lot of pictures. When you come to print out, you may find you use a lot of black ink – and ink cartridges are quite an expensive consumable item! If you do not want to print out the pictures, you can set your computer to download text only – you will also find that they load much more quickly.

Disciplining yourself

When you log on to the net, you can be tempted to wander wherever the fancy takes you. When you are looking something up, all sorts of other interesting sites are suggested, either by links from the site you are looking at, or by a search engine.

When you go on to the Internet for a session, decide just what you want from that session. If you are looking for something specific, go straight to it, and do not let yourself be diverted. If you are finding out more about a subject, you may want to wander. At all events, set yourself a time limit.

Communicating

The Internet is not just the World Wide Web. It is a way of communicating with others. Your Internet Service Provider will have some channels to 'chat rooms'. These are spaces where you can talk to other people about your favourite subject, or a subject of the moment. These chat rooms have different topics, and practically all the channels have chat rooms devoted to money matters.

Many of the e-zines and other sites have bulletin boards, where you can post messages, which will provoke responses from other users.

You can think of these bulletin boards or chat rooms as 'cyber investment clubs' where you can exchange tips or the latest information. But you must use common sense. The site operators always disclaim any responsibility for information posted on bulletin boards or chat rooms. Some people have tried to use these resources to post misleading information, and thereby manipulate prices of shares. Learn to judge the quality of the information.

Have fun!

The Internet is dynamic, interesting and fun. It is a relatively new technology, and is constantly changing.

There is a steep learning curve involved – but once you are up and running, you will find your own way around the Internet. You will find it is an unrivalled source of information.

2

Security and Regulation on the Internet

The Internet can be a great place to get all sorts of information about investments – and about money matters in general. Always bear in mind, however, that the companies with web sites use them as marketing tools. They want you to buy their products. In addition, of course, the Internet is an ideal place for all sorts of frauds and scams.

Always bear in mind the golden rule – if something looks too good to be true, it probably is. However, when buying goods or services of any sort over the Internet, you cannot physically see or handle what you are buying. Always make absolutely sure exactly what it is that you are buying. If you do not understand a description, ask for more information. Any reputable company will give you all the information about their products or services. This includes such things as:

- delivery dates

- return of goods

- 'cooling-off' periods during which you have the right to change your mind

- guarantees.

Not long ago, www.new-utopia.com attracted many people to invest over the Internet. It promised citizenship of a new 'principality' to be built on a chain of coral reefs in the Caribbean. The US Securities and Exchange Commission (SEC) shut it down, and froze all the assets, after judging it to be fraudulent.

The SEC in the USA and the British Financial Services Authority regulate investment business. They are always on the lookout for frauds perpetrated through the Internet.

There are also independent and government sites which look out for fraud and scams.

REGULATORY AND GOVERNMENT BODIES

The Bank of England   www.bankofengland.co.uk

This is the ultimate regulator of all banking activity in the UK. Its web site is informative, but you would probably need to know much about economics and finance to understand all of the press releases, publications, etc. However, for the more casual browser, there is the section about the museum, with much of interest.

Financial Services Authority   www.sib.co.uk

This body used to be called the Securities and Investments Board – hence the web site address. It is the regulatory body for the financial services authority, and it has government backing.

The site tells you all about how the industry is regulated, and how to contact the FSA if you need to. It has a page called 'Investor alerts'. Some recent ones include:

- *Warning on telephone scam.* Be on your guard against telephone callers who pose as bank or building society officials and ask for your account details, in an attempt to get at your money.

- *Have you lost out on your pension?* Information about the pensions mis-selling scandal.

- *Warning on 'copycat' sites.* Make sure you don't get taken in by bogus web sites.

- *Investing over the Internet: a one-minute exercise.* This page takes 60 seconds to read, but could save you a fortune.

This is a well-designed site, and user friendly.

The Insurance Ombudsman Bureau   www.thejob.org.uk

This is the site of an organisation set up by the insurance industry to resolve disputes between the public and insurance companies. It should, of course, only be used if you cannot first resolve the dispute with the company itself.

You can send a complaint by email, and they will tell you the correct procedure to follow.

| **The London Stock Exchange** | www.londonstockex.co.uk |

This is the official site of the London Stock Exchange. It will tell you almost anything you want to know about the Exchange and its members.

| **Office of Fair Trading** | www.oft.gov.uk |

The OFT is a British Government department. The web site gives links to various other organisations around the world working for fair trade and consumer protection. You can operate a wordsearch on this site, to find references to your subject in speeches, official leaflets, etc.

The OFT site has information to help you understand financial products, such as mortgages (see Figure 1).

Fig. 1. Office of Fair Trading Guide to Personal Finance.

| **Occupational Pensions Regulatory Authority** | www.opra.gov.uk |

This body regulates company pension schemes, making sure they are properly run, and the funds properly invested. There is a pension-tracing service, which may help you to track down a company pension you have lost.

MEMBERSHIP BODIES

These are bodies which have a membership, and can exercise some kind of discipline and regulatory oversight of the members.

The Annuity Bureau	www.annuity-bureau.co.uk

This organisation provides information about pensions and annuities.

Association of British Insurers	www.abi.org

This is the body for insurance companies, and pension companies. It has a consumer information service.

Association of Unit Trust and Investment Funds (AUTIF)	www.investmentfunds.org.uk

Association of Investment Trust Companies (AITC)	www.aitc.co.uk

Institute of Financial Planning	www.financialplanning.org.uk

Independent Financial Advisers Association (IFAA)	www.ifaa.org.uk

IFA Promotion Ltd	www.unbiased.co.uk

This is actually an organisation that promotes independent financial advisers. They will send you the names and addresses of three local independent financial advisers, and a voucher for a free 'no obligation' consultation.

The National Association of Pension Funds	www.napf.co.uk

This site is designed for pension fund managers, and it can provide information on legislation affecting pensions.

The Pensions Advisory Service	www.opas.org.uk

This site explains the powers of the organisation. It can help in disputes or sorting out problems with pension schemes.

WATCHDOG BODIES

Advertising Standards Authority	www.asa.org.uk

This organisation monitors advertisements, whether on the Internet or not. It offers advice to consumers, and carries weight with commercial advertisers. Its aim is to ensure that advertisements are legal, decent, honest and truthful. It is an independent body, and although not a government organisation, it does have certain powers. Its scope covers advertisements and promotions in non-broadcast media. This includes things like newspaper and magazine advertisements, hoardings, competitions and prize draws.

The web site gives a summary of all its adjudications, listed each month.

Offshore Alert	www.offshorebusiness.com

Stock Detective	www.stockdetective.com

This is an American site, so its references are mainly to American investments. It highlights how unscrupulous manipulators can 'rig' share prices to their own benefit. The specifics are not exclusively Internet based, but they are mainly American. It is worth a visit to this site.

Internet Scam Busters	www.scambusters.com

This is another American site, and it is in the form of an e-zine. You will have to register, but it is free of charge. There is a large range of articles about various types of Internet fraud. Again, it is worth a visit, to put you on your guard. The types of fraud are changing all the time, and subscribers to this e-zine keep it up to date.

Internet Fraud Watch	www.fraud.org

Yet another American site – this time the web site of the National Consumers League. This is an American consumers' organisation, which is updated by its members on frauds and scams of all kinds.

Moneyweb	www.moneyweb.co.uk

This site has several articles about current scams and cons. There is also a 'guide for educated cynics' about how to read the performance statistics published by insurance and investment companies – and how not to be misled by them.

The Plain English Campaign   www.plainenglish.co.uk

This site and organisation does not have an explicitly 'watchdog' function, but encourages organisations of all kinds to use plain, simple English. It awards its 'crystal mark' for good examples. It also publishes guides, one of which is a guide to pensions. This can be helpful in cutting through the jargon to understand this subject properly.

Standard and Poors   www.standardandpoors.com

This is the leading company for assessing and rating various financial organisations. Its ratings give an indication of the creditworthiness of companies, and the general reliability of funds such as unit trusts or investment trusts. If a fund or company has a high rating, it is sure to make much of this in its advertising, and on its web site. The ratings are universally regarded as one of the best independent sources.

CREDIT CARD AND BANKING SECURITY

One of the concerns about doing business on the Internet is the security of credit card information. On the whole, provided the company you are dealing with has secured their site, security is at least as good as, if not better than, using your credit card over the telephone.

The security of this information comes by means of encryption. This is a way of 'scrambling' any information sent via a certain page of a web site. It can then only be unscrambled by the genuine receiver of the information. This service should be available with any company which expects you to place an order for goods or services over the Internet. It is also, of course, an essential part of Internet banking procedure.

In the final analysis, the security of your credit card details rests with the company you are dealing with. It makes sense, then, to satisfy yourself that they are who they claim to be. A common ploy of fraudsters is to register a web site with a similar name to one which is well known. In addition, registration of a 'domain name' (the web site) can be made in one country, while the actual person or company is in a different country. Make sure you know the geographical address of the company you are dealing with.

Encryption is offered on current versions of the browsers from Netscape Navigator and Internet Explorer. A small padlock icon in the bottom left-hand corner of the screen indicates 40-bit encryption,

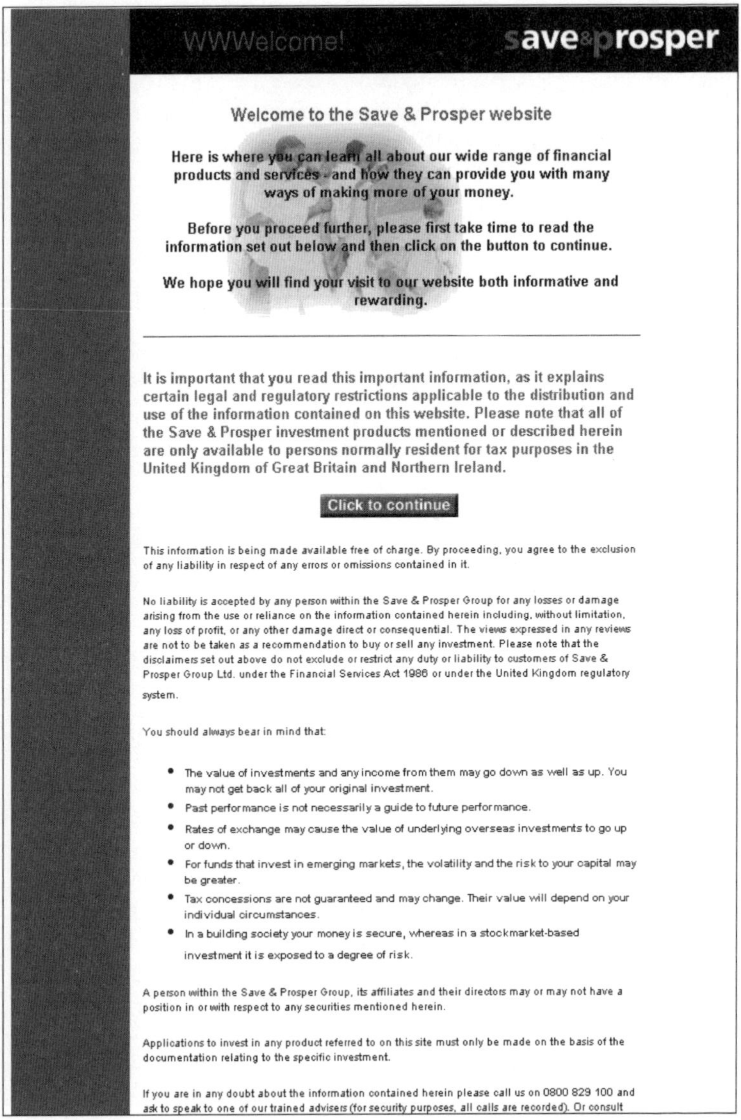

Fig. 2. Save and Prosper entry page.

and a large padlock icon indicates 128-bit encryption (a higher level of encryption).

> **Remember – if in doubt, don't.**

LEGAL AND REGULATORY RESTRICTIONS

The law requires firms offering investment advice to observe certain restrictions, such as to provide risk warnings to customers, to say whether or not they are giving independent financial advice, and so on. Some web sites (such as Save and Prosper – see Figure 2) have a page of these legalities which you must click before you can progress any further. If you click to progress, you are accepting the terms and conditions, and acknowledging that you have read all the conditions and restrictions.

CHECKLIST

1. Always be wary of something that sounds too good to be true.

2. If you are buying goods or services, make sure that you know the company you are dealing with, and that you have all the information you need.

3. If you are giving your credit card or bank details, make sure the connection is secure.

4. You can check with regulatory bodies or watchdog bodies if you are unsure.

3

Savings Sites

In this book, 'savings' refers to accounts which will pay you interest in one form or another. Other types of investments, such as stocks and shares, are dealt with as 'investments'.

A planned savings and investment strategy should always leave room for some money to be invested to gain interest, with a major factor being the period of notice required to get at your money. When looking for a home for your savings, do not just concentrate on the headline interest rate. Look for the period of notice required, the size and security of the provider, and the ease of operation – for instance, is it an Internet-only account, or can you access the money at a local branch?

Banks and building societies, and many of the insurance companies, offer savings accounts. However, the first site to look at is:

NATIONAL SAVINGS

National Savings	www.nationalsavings.co.uk

Yes, this address *is* correct. Although National Savings is a government department, it has a co.uk address. The home page has fancy graphics, and you are warned that to best experience the site you need **shockwave** – you can download it in about ten minutes from the site.

Even without shockwave, the site has a modern look and feel. You can go to various pages of the site, to see the different types of products. For each page there is a 'toolbox'. This has several 'tools' including:

- calculator
- jargon buster
- tax information
- common questions
- contact us.

If you have premium bonds, and you want to check if you have an unclaimed prize, you can enter your holder's number (not the actual bond number) and it will tell you if you have an unclaimed prize.

There is a press release page, intended mainly for journalists, and an IFA page, intended mainly for financial intermediaries.

The site, of course, gives details of all the National Savings products. There is bound to be at least one which will suit your circumstances.

BANKS AND BUILDING SOCIETIES

Abbey National	www.abbeynational.co.uk

They offer a direct savings account, for a minimum of £2,000.

Barclays Bank	www.personal.barclays.co.uk

This large bank offers many savings accounts, including:

- Easy Access
- Longer Term
- Tax Efficient.

There is a beginners' guide, with advice to help you, whether you are a taxpayer or not.

Cheltenham & Gloucester	www.cheltglos.co.uk

(See Figure 3.) This society was taken over by Lloyds Bank in 1995. It offers the following:

- Direct Transfer Account
- Branch 10
- Direct 30
- 90 Day Account
- C&G London Account
- Cheltenham Gold
- C&G Cash ISA
- C&G TESSA ISA
- C&G Tracker.

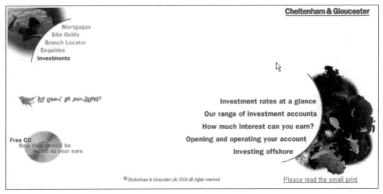

Fig. 3. Cheltenham & Gloucester investments page.

Chesham Building Society   www.cheshambsoc.co.uk

This old-established building society offers savings accounts as follows:

- Instant Access
- Young Savers
- Postal Account
- ISAs
- Notice Accounts.

Branch-based accounts are only available to people living in the local area, but the postal accounts are more widely available.

Co-operative Bank   www.co-operativebank.co.uk

This bank offers:

- Pathfinder Account
- Instant Access Account with debit card
- Save Direct Account
- ISA
- Guaranteed Investment Bond
- Online Application Forms.

Egg   www.egg.com

This is the Internet banking arm of Prudential. Egg accounts can only be opened and operated through the Internet. The savings account can be opened with as little as £1, one of very few to offer this feature. The interest rate is competitive, with no notice for withdrawals, and is slightly higher if you choose to operate your account via the Internet only. There is a slightly lower rate of interest on the account if you choose to have cash card access to your savings.

Halifax   www.halifax.co.uk

As you would expect from the largest of the demutualised building societies, there are a number of accounts catering for:

- easy access
- notice accounts
- regular savings
- fixed interest.

You can take the Halifax's '10-minute saving review' to check your needs.

HSBC   www.hsbc.co.uk

This bank offers:

- simple savings
- longer-term savings
- tax-free savings
- children's savings
- savings for larger amounts.

Lambeth Building Society   www.simplypostal.co.uk

This is a mutual building society which is keen to retain its mutual status. To discourage carpetbaggers, it operates a 'charitable assignment' scheme. All new savers opening share accounts must agree to assign any future windfall rights to the Charities Aid Foundation for the first five years of their membership of the Society. They also have special accounts for supporters of Queens Park Rangers Football

Club, and Tottenham Hotspur Football Club. Their savings accounts include:

- Simply Fixed Rate Share
- ISA
- TESSA Transfer
- Postal 30 Share
- Postal 180 Share.

Leeds and Holbeck Building Society   www. leeds-holbeck.co.uk

---

This society has a range of savings accounts, including a special one for supporters of Leeds United Football Club. There is also a 'Charity Care' account. This account supports three nominated charities – Save the Children, Marie Curie Cancer Care and Help the Aged. You get interest on your account, and a range of extra benefits. In addition, the society gives 1 per cent of the average balance on the account to the charities – shared equally. Here is the full range of their accounts:

- 50 + Saver
- Fixed Rate Bonds (1, 2, 3 and 4 year bonds)
- Share Linked Bond
- Charity Care
- Premier Current
- Leeds United
- ISAs
- Postal Accounts
- Capital 7 Account
- Regular Saver Account
- Portfolio Gold
- Premium Access.

Lloyds TSB Bank   www.lloydstsb.co.uk

This bank has:

- 90-day notice accounts
- flexible savings accounts
- classic current accounts with interest
- Instant Gold savings accounts
- cash ISAs
- premier gold accounts

- regular savings accounts
- select savings accounts
- term deposit accounts
- young savers' accounts.

Nationwide Building Society   www.nationwide.co.uk

This is an attractive site, dealing with the core business of the Nationwide in banking, mortgages, savings, insurance and personal loans.

The site also has features on the Nationwide football league, a chance to win £500 to spend at Marks and Spencer, entertainment, shopping, travel, sport and Internet access.

NatWest Bank   www.natwest.co.uk

This is one of the big banks. Savings accounts on offer include:

- First Reserve – instant access and optional cash card
- Premium Reserve – instant access with higher interest for amounts over £2,000
- Reward Reserve – instant access with the potential to earn extra interest
- Diamond Reserve – one month's notice required if you are withdrawing more than £250
- Crown Reserve – minimum £50,000, with 3 months' notice for withdrawals over £250 per month
- Millennium Bond – two-year term bond with minimum £2,000
- Personal Savings Bond – five-year term bond with minimum £5,000
- Young Saver – instant access for under-11s
- Personal Savings Bond for Children – five-year term bond with minimum £1,000
- Community Bond – one- or three-year term bond where some or all of the interest can be paid towards community projects.

Newcastle Building Society   www.newcastle.co.uk

The Newcastle has a choice of savings accounts, some of which do not require any notice of withdrawal, and some of which do. There are various special accounts also, and the full range includes:

- Nova Plus

- Nova Access Direct
- Portfolio Plus
- Nova 18
- Nova ISA
- Nova ISA Direct
- TESSA only ISA
- Fixed Rate ISA
- The Key Account
- Offshore Savings.

Royal Bank of Scotland   www.rbs.co.uk

This has several accounts including an Internet-operated account. There is also an account which links the interest on a seven-year term savings account to house prices. The interest is only paid at the end of the seven years, and is equal to 1.4 times the growth of the Halifax House Prices Index over the seven-year term. The full range is:

- Direct Saver (Internet account)
- Instant Access Savings Account
- Gold Deposit Account
- 30 Day Savings Account
- 60 Day Savings Account
- Bonus 90 Account
- Instant Access ISA
- 60 Day ISA
- Guaranteed Income Account
- House Price Linked Savings Account.

Standard Life Bank   www.standardlifebank.com

On offer here:

- 50 Day Notice Account
- Business Saving Account
- Client Account for professionals
- Direct Access Account.

Skipton Building Society   www.skipton.co.uk

This society has several accounts, including:

- Web Exclusive Bond

- 2-Year Step-Up Bond
- Roses Investment Account
- 3-Year Fixed Rate Bond
- Young Sovereign Share
- Base Rate Tracker
- Bonus Portfolio
- Mini Cash ISA for NSPCC
- Lifestyle ISA
- TESSA only ISA
- Offshore Investments.

Teachers Building Society   www.teachersbs.co.uk

This society has several accounts to cater for different requirements such as easy access, specific notice requirements (30 days or 60 days), monthly interest, postal accounts, regular savings and ISAs.

Triodos Bank   www.triodos.co.uk

This 'ethical' bank has savings accounts for differing notice requirements:

- Instant
- 33 Days' Notice
- Long Term.

There are also 'special needs' accounts for:

- children and young people
- regular savings
- monthly income
- tax-free savings
- targeting money to particular sectors.

Woolwich   www.woolwich.co.uk

This is one of the larger demutualised building societies. It has a large range of savings accounts, including:

Current Account	Woolwich for Kids Club
Card Saver	Maturity Options Account
Direct Access	Premier Bonus Account
ISAVE Card Saver	6 Month Fixed Rate Bond
ISA Cash (variable rate)	1 Year Fixed Rate Bond

Prime Gold	2 Year Fixed Rate Bond
Premier Instant	5 Year Fixed Rate Bond
Premier 30	3 Year Guaranteed Growth Bond
Premier 90	Base Rate Tracker Bond
Premier Plus	Charlton Premier Savings Account

INSURANCE COMPANIES

Many insurance companies promote what they call 'savings plans' on their web sites. Many of these are, in fact, life assurance policies or bonds with a savings element.

Direct Line   www.directline.com

This company offers a 'Direct Access Account' with competitive rates of interest, tiered according to the amount in the account. 'Direct Access' means deposits and withdrawals are done within three working days, to or from a nominated external bank account.

Equitable Life   www.equitable.co.uk

This web site includes a section to help you decide what sort of savings account you need. It does this by prompting you to think about your attitude to risk, identifying your family and work circumstances, and establishing your objectives. A 'route map' then guides you through the choices available. The savings plans they offer are all either life assurance policies or unit trusts, with an ISA option. Of course, you can use their 'route map' to help you decide, but apply the principles to other companies and other forms of savings.

Legal & General   www.landg.com

This company offers a term savings account with a guaranteed interest rate for twelve months.

Norwich Union   www.norwich-union.co.uk

Norwich Union offers regular savings and lump sum investment plans, with an ISA option. However, the company does also offer a deposit account facility in conjunction with Bank of Scotland. This is a 'savings tracker' account. The interest on this account will beat or match the average interest rate of twelve other leading deposit account providers. There are tiered interest rates according to the amount invested.

Prudential www.pru.co.uk

This site gives details of the savings accounts it offers. Its Internet banking arm is Egg (an Internet-only service). This site gives details of its 'normal' banking facilities. Savings accounts include:

- High Interest Deposit
- 60 Day Account
- Gold ISA
- Investment Bond
- Unit Trusts.

Royal Liver Assurance www.royal-liver.com

There are plans for regular savings or lump sum investments, which are all life assurance plans.

Sun Life of Canada www.slocpensions.co.uk

The site describes what they call 'savings plans'. These are life assurance products, geared to either regular savings or lump sum investment.

OTHER PROVIDERS

Marks and Spencer www.marks-and-spencer.co.uk

This is, of course, the famous retailer. Like others, it has introduced financial services to its product range. There is not a great choice of savings accounts compared with other financial institutions, but it is worth a look.

Tesco Personal Finance www.tesco.co.uk

This retailer has a savings account as part of its personal financial services. This instant access savings account pays a competitive rate of interest, which Tesco compares with other instant access accounts. Access to your savings can be by telephone (24-hour service) or a cash card at cash machines at Tesco shops.

INDEPENDENT ADVICE

Interactive Investor International	www.iii.co.uk

This site has a page called 'Savings Centre', showing the top rates of interest given for various types of savings accounts, such as:

- No Notice Accounts
- Notice Accounts
- Monthly Interest
- Cheque Accounts
- Mini Cash ISAs
- Fixed Rate Bonds
- Guaranteed Income Bonds.

Moneywise	www.moneywise.co.uk

This is a magazine which has a section on savings, to give you all the latest details about savings rates.

Money World	www.moneyworld.co.uk

This is an e-zine, which can give you the latest rates and 'best buys', when you click on the savings section.

4

Getting a Mortgage on the Internet

A house is probably the largest single purchase you will make in your life. How can you use the Internet to help you get a mortgage? Before we look at the Internet, let's look at the principles of mortgage lending.

FINANCING YOUR HOME

If you are lucky enough to be able to pay cash for your house, stop reading here. However, most of us ordinary mortals have to raise some finance to buy a house. A loan that is secured on the property is called a mortgage. There are many suppliers of mortgage finance. The commonest are banks, building societies and insurance companies, most of which have their own web sites and email addresses.

When we say that a loan is 'secured', that means that the lender has a legal title to the property, in the case of your failing to meet the repayments. This is why advertisements for mortgage products and loans carry the risk warning 'Your home is at risk if you do not keep up the repayments'.

When buying a house, you first decide how much you can afford. This is determined not only by the price of the house itself, but by how much deposit you can put down, and how much you can afford as regular repayments. There are several factors to bear in mind:

- loan to valuation
- income multiplier
- length of expected occupancy.

Loan to valuation

When you want a mortgage, the lender will value the house. The value they put on it may have no relationship at all to the price you pay for the house. They must always look at the 'worst case scenario'. If you could not keep up the repayments, they would have to repossess the house and sell it to get back the money they loaned you. Therefore, the value is an important factor for them.

The lender appoints their own valuer. This is normally someone from your area, who knows local conditions. The lenders have a panel of valuers for each area. You will have to pay the costs of that valuation, which is purely a valuation for the purposes of the mortgage advance. You have the option to pay a little more and get a homebuyer's report, or a full structural survey from the same valuer. You can, of course, get a surveyor of your own to do the job.

The amount you want to borrow is then considered as a percentage of the valuation figure. Thus, if they valued the house at £100,000, and you wanted to borrow £90,000, the loan to valuation is said to be 90 per cent. In the heady days of the mid-1980s, lenders were giving up to 100 per cent of the values, and too often these valuations were to prove optimistic when property prices crashed. This led to the 'negative equity' problem which plagued many people's lives. However, there are still some 100 per cent mortgages available.

The loan to valuation affects the interest rate. A higher rate of interest is the price for a higher loan to value ratio.

A high loan to valuation percentage will also trigger a Mortgage Indemnity Guarantee (MIG) requirement. This means that the lender will require you to pay an insurance premium against the possibility that you will not be able to repay them if the property has to be sold. This is an attempt to avoid the 'negative equity' problem. You may have to find the premium up front, from your own resources, but sometimes this can be added to the amount of the mortgage advance.

Income multiplier

The lender wants to be sure you can repay the mortgage. The amount you want to borrow is expressed as a 'multiplier' of your income. Thus, if your income is £15,000 per year, and you want to borrow £30,000, the income multiplier is said to be 2 times. Lenders have their own limits for income multipliers.

A typical income multiplier for a single person might be 3.5 times income. For a couple it might be expressed as the higher of:

- 3.5 times first income plus 1 times second income, *or*
- 2.75 times joint income.

The higher income is considered as the first income.

Example:
Husband's income £18,000 per year.
Wife's income £10,000 per year.

3.5 times first income	=	£63,000
1 times second income	=	£10,000
Total		£73,000

2.75 times joint income = £77,000

The maximum loan on this basis would be £77,000.

If the income multiplier and the loan to valuation figures are not the same, the amount they would be willing to loan is the lower of the two figures.

Most lenders' web sites include a 'ready reckoner' of some sort. You can key in your details – income, price of house, age, etc. You will then get an answer of the sort of mortgage you could get, and the monthly repayments.

Question and answer

I cannot quite make up the figure I want to borrow. Why not start doing more overtime, or moonlighting, to increase my earnings, and qualify for a bigger mortgage?

The income multiplier is meant to determine how much you could comfortably repay on a regular basis. It is there to protect you, the borrower, as much as the lender. If you earn more by overtime or moonlighting, are you going to be able to keep up the pace? Think about this very carefully. You are the one most likely to suffer.

Length of expected occupancy

When considering how much you could afford, apart from taking into account the loan criteria, you should also consider how long you expect to be in the house. You may know that you will be moving on in a few years' time, either because you will need a bigger house as a family comes along, or because of a geographical move. That will obviously affect your decision about the house, whether you expect to do major improvements, etc. It will also affect your decision about the term of the mortgage, i.e. the number of years over which it is to be repaid.

REPAYING THE MORTGAGE

Over time, lenders have developed many different ways of allowing you to repay the mortgage.

The simplest is the **repayment mortgage**. This means that you make monthly repayments which include a part for the interest, and a part for the capital. This is worked out according to the term of the loan and the interest rate prevailing when you borrow the money.

Any subsequent changes in the interest rate mean that the monthly repayment has to be altered.

Mortgage protection insurance

Normally, the bank or building society would also require a life assurance protection policy to be taken out. If you die before you have paid off the mortgage, the life assurance would pay off the balance owing. (The lender is naturally uneasy about the prospect of repossessing a house and having to throw out a recently widowed person.)

Interest-only repayments

There are various form of 'interest-only' repayment plans. This means that the monthly repayment is for interest only. The capital is not repaid monthly, but by means of a savings plan of some sort. The most usual are:

- endowment mortgages
- pension mortgages
- PEP and ISA mortgages.

Endowment mortgages
An endowment mortgage means that you take out an endowment life assurance policy for the term of the loan, and for the amount you borrowed. You make the normal premiums to the life assurance company. When the term of the mortgage is over, the life assurance policy matures, and the money is used to repay the capital of the mortgage. This also provides the life assurance protection to repay the mortgage if you die in the meantime.

Pension mortgages
Under this scheme, you take out a personal pension policy. When the pension policy matures, you take the maximum tax-free lump sum to repay the mortgage. This type of policy attracts tax relief at your top

rate of tax, so you could, at present tax rates, get up to 40 per cent tax relief. However, only 25 per cent of the fund may be taken as a tax-free lump sum, so that the funding needs to be at least four times the mortgage to ensure that the mortgage can be repaid. The earliest a policy could mature is age 50, so the term of the mortgage could not end before that date.

PEP and ISA mortgages
A PEP mortgage was a scheme whereby, in addition to the interest payments monthly, you invested in a PEP (a tax-free investment). This then accumulated a fund to repay the mortgage at the end of the term. PEPs are no longer available (since April 1999). The new form of tax-free saving is called ISA (Individual Savings Account), and there are ISA mortgages now on offer.

Lifestyle mortgages (also known as 'flexible' or 'accelerator' mortgages)
The most recent form of mortgage is a 'hybrid' between a conventional bank account and a mortgage. The idea of this is that you make maximum use of the loan facility. As long as your borrowing does not exceed your overall limit, you may operate your account as a bank account, and make use of the loan facility in any way you like. Your normal credits to your account (e.g. your monthly salary) are credited to this account, and your normal expenditure is charged to this account. Legal & General and Virgin offer this type of mortgage.

The principle behind this account is that interest is calculated with daily rests (see page 39), and therefore you make the optimum use of the timing of your credits to the account, and the payments out of it. This type of account is also sometimes known as an 'accelerator' mortgage, because you can pay it off quicker.

INTEREST RATES

Banks and building societies have been very competitive in recent years, and now offer a range of interest types, including discounts, cashbacks, tracker rates and fixed interest rates.

Discounts
Discounts are offered, some to first-time buyers, and some as a simple incentive to persuade borrowers to change their mortgage lender.

These discounts represent a cheaper interest rate for a fixed period, typically one, two or three years.

Cashbacks

Cashbacks are also offered as an incentive. The cashback will typically be a percentage of the amount borrowed, up to a certain maximum figure. There are many ways in which lenders offer cashbacks. The most straightforward is, as the name suggests, a cash refund to the borrower when the mortgage is finalised. However, some lenders offer it as a bonus after a certain number of years, which will be used to reduce the mortgage debt. Others pay it in the form of vouchers which can be used to make the repayments on the mortgage at some time in the future.

Penalties

Both discounts and cashbacks are subject to penalties, i.e. repayment of the amount saved or repaid, if the mortgage is repaid within a certain time limit – usually five years.

Tracker rates

These mortgages guarantee to charge interest rates that track the movement in base interest rates. Interest rates on normal variable rate loans do tend to follow base rate movements, but tracker rates have a promise to follow base rates within a set time period.

Fixed interest

Fixed interest rates are also given as an incentive. These are rates of interest that are guaranteed to stay the same for a given period. At the expiry of this period, the interest rate reverts to the normal variable interest rate. Some lenders offer fixed interest rates for a limited period as well as a cashback on the same loan.

CHARGING PERIODS

In looking at the 'lifestyle' or 'accelerator' mortgages mentioned above, we saw that they were based on interest being charged with daily rests. This is a key factor, and one which many people overlook. It is easy to consider only the actual interest rate, without thinking about the effect of the charging period. This can have a profound effect on the actual amount you pay, irrespective of the interest rate.

Interest calculation period

If interest is calculated in advance with yearly rests, this means that it is calculated on the amount of the loan outstanding at the beginning of the year. The same interest is charged for the rest of the year, regardless of what you do to the account during that year. Thus you get no benefit at all for paying off some of the mortgage during the course of the year.

At the other end of the scale, if interest is calculated with daily rests, it is calculated on each day's balance at a daily rate (the annual interest rate divided by 365). Thus, if you are able to pay off some of the mortgage, the interest starts to reduce as soon as you reduce the mortgage.

Interest charging period

The interval of charging the interest to the account can make a significant difference. If, for example, interest is charged to the account monthly, then each time interest is added, the balance on which the next interest is calculated also increases. This therefore further increases the next interest amount. The effect is cumulative.

However, if interest is only added to the account once a year, then in the intervening twelve months, the interest calculation is lower, because the interest has not been cumulative.

Therefore, look for the longest possible interval of charging interest to the mortgage, and the shortest possible period of calculating interest – daily if possible.

SPECIAL CASES

Special cases, i.e. not a simple residential mortgage, are treated differently by the mortgage lender. This is because the risk profile is perceived as being different. You can find specialist lenders for special cases on the Internet.

Impaired credit

If you are currently in arrears with any debt repayment, or if you have a county court judgement (ccj) against you, the mortgage lender will discover this when they do a credit search. Another problem can arise where, for some reason, you are unable to produce full proof of your income. This is known as 'non-status lending'.

Many lenders will see these problems as the end of the road, and tell you that they cannot make you an offer of a mortgage. However, there are some lenders who specialise in this type of lending (known as 'impaired credit lending', or 'non-status lending').

Negative equity

If you have negative equity, it can be almost impossible to get a mortgage to move house, and you may feel trapped. Cheltenham & Gloucester provide a mortgage to help in this circumstance. Legal & General do not tackle negative equity, but they do provide a 100 per cent mortgage for home-owners with no equity.

Commercial mortgages

These are mortgages on property, not for private residential purposes, but for running a business, such as a shop, public house or hotel, or a workshop. The lender is therefore lending money to finance a business, and sharing to a certain extent in the risk of the business. The lender therefore approaches a commercial mortgage in a different way. A large part of their enquiries will be about the way the business is or will be run, and your ability to run it. They will look at your business plan, including profit and cashflow forecasts. Several lenders offer this facility.

Some property will be part private residential, and part business. This would include properties such as pubs, or shops with living accommodation above, and so on.

Buying to let

You may want to buy a residential property not to live in yourself, but to let out to tenants. This is not quite the same as a commercial property, but similar risks will attach to this kind of property, and therefore the mortgage. For example, there is the possibility that a tenant may leave, and you are not able to re-let the property for some time. How could you keep up the repayments in that case? What if the tenant leaves the property in a bad state of repair or decoration? Legal & General are one company to offer this type of mortgage.

Self-build mortgages

If you are building your own house, you may be able to get a mortgage to finance it. The finance is only paid in stages, as your building project progresses. Bradford & Bingley offer finance for this sort of project.

Right to buy

If you are seeking a mortgage for your council house under the 'right to buy' scheme, this may need special consideration by the lender. Bradford & Bingley have mortgages for this.

Foreign currency mortgages

It may be possible to get a mortgage in a foreign currency, where interest rates are lower. Of course, you should always bear in mind that exchange rates fluctuate, and to repay the mortgage may still prove more costly because of these fluctuations, and costs of converting money to another currency.

The Abbey National offers a Euro mortgage for people not paid in sterling currency.

WEB SITES

Office of Fair Trading   www.oft.gov.uk/html/finance

The Office of Fair Trading has a web site, and this part is devoted to a personal finance guide.

The section dealing with mortgages starts with a brief introduction to mortgages for the absolute beginner. Further sections deal with repayment mortgages, endowment mortgages, PEP and ISA mortgages, making your choice of mortgage, and points to look out for. These include such things as not over-extending yourself, and knowing whether you have to take other services such as insurance as a condition of the mortgage.

This site is, of course, genuinely independent, and tells you what to look out for, pitfalls to avoid, and general hints.

I thoroughly recommend a visit before you look at any other sites – in fact, before you start the business of applying for a mortgage.

Financial Information Net Directory   www.find.co.uk

This site offers links to many other sites. It is owned by Omnium Communications Ltd. The home page gives you options for several aspects of financial information, one of which is mortgages and loans. Under this section you can go to:

- mortgage lenders
- mortgage rates and brokers
- personal loans
- commercial finance
- credit cards.

This site is a good jumping-off point to search for a mortgage.

Building societies and other mortgage lenders

Most lenders have a presence on the net, and display their own products, with some form of general mortgage information.

The larger lenders have a lot of information in their sites, reflecting the range of products they provide. Most of them have something special on their site, such as a prize draw, 'Charity Care' (the Leeds and Holbeck), share-dealing service, news of take-over activity or demutualisation, etc. Most include:

- an interactive reckoner, to tell you what the monthly repayments would be on a mortgage of a certain size
- a guide to mortgages, moving house, or explanation of mortgage jargon
- a branch finder or directory, to tell you the nearest branch to you
- a response section for you to make enquiries or an application by email
- information on the various types of mortgages – cashbacks, discounted, fixed rates, capped rates, etc.
- some comment on the mutuality issue from societies which have not converted
- latest news from the lender.

If you have already made your choice of lender through one of the other means, you can then access the lender through their web site and make your application.

Here are some of the lenders on the web:

Abbey National plc	www.abbeynational.co.uk

The home page, as you would expect from a large lender, offers many services besides mortgages. It has a large feature on the Euro – and what it means to you. This links with their service for Euro mortgages.

The mortgages home page sorts you out between first-time buyers, moving home, moving your mortgage to the Abbey National, and reviewing your existing mortgage. Clicking on the different options will take you by different routes, but you'll finish up with the same information, i.e. a summary of the types of mortgage available.

There is also information on the insurance products covering mortgages. These are:

- Paymentcare – an illness insurance to cover your repayments
- mortgage protection – life cover to pay off the mortgage on death.

Birmingham Midshires Building Society   www.worldserver.pipex.com/bmbs

This is a simple, no-frills site.

The mortgage page shows a text-only list of all the current mortgage products. They do not appear to have an 'ordinary' variable-rate mortgage – the only ones listed are discounted, fixed rates, or capped. There is no interactive calculator.

There is nothing exciting about this as a web site, but if you want to find out their rates and products, they are set out clearly and simply.

Bradford & Bingley Building Society   www.bradford-bingley.co.uk

The 'home buying' option is the section dealing with mortgages. You can click on first-time buyer, moving house, moving your mortgage, specialised mortgages, and ask for their 'useful guides'. This is a simple, straightforward site.

Cheltenham & Gloucester   www.cheltglos.co.uk

The home page includes links to Lloyds TSB Bank – all part of the same group. You can also have the chance to win one of 50 free CDs in the survey, and download a screensaver from the home page.

The mortgages section has information on their products. As expected, these include the usual variations. They also have two innovative products:

- An airmiles mortgage (you can get airmiles instead of cashback).
- A negative equity mortgage. This gives you a loan up to 120 per cent of valuation to move house if you have negative equity.

The Cheltenham & Gloucester have an imaginative range of mortgage products and their web site is well designed, with incentives to browse.

Chesham Building Society   www.cheshambsoc.co.uk

This society prides itself on being the oldest building society in the country, and emphasises the fact that it only deals with mortgages and savings. The web site is well designed, with easy links to and from each section, and response forms to apply for mortgages. The society emphasises that it only offers mortgages up to 80 per cent of valuation, except in its local post code area, where it could advance up to 95 per cent.

This is a traditional society with conservative values, reflected in its site.

Halifax pic   www.halifax.co.uk

This is the big one! As you would expect from a company as big as this, the web site is crammed full of information on a wide range of products and activities. The mortgage section gives details of their mortgage deals.

They claim that their Home Arranger service is unique, 'taking the hassle out of moving home'. Perhaps the most innovative feature is the 'mix and match' option. This means that you can take part of your mortgage at a fixed rate, part discounted, and part with cash-back. This site is well worth a visit if you are looking for a mortgage, or even just to browse.

Lambeth Building Society   www.simplypostal.co.uk

This site allows you to e-mail the Lambeth to join their mailing list. You may also request a 'mortgage decision in principle' request form. They also display their fixed, discounted or capped rates, and the remortgage deals with free fees.

Leeds and Holbeck Building Society   www. leeds-holbeck.co.uk

---

This is a mutual building society, which makes the point in its web site that it wants to stay that way.

The mortgage section points you to details on fixed rates, discounts, cashback, fee free, buy to let, shared ownership, and an explanation of mortgage jargon.

The cashback deal is one of the best around, giving cashback of 1 per cent every year for five years. However, don't forget to check out the interest rates.

The shared ownership mortgage scheme allows you to buy a share of the property you want, and could be a good step to owning your own property outright. However, the web site offers very little information about this scheme. You'll have to go to one of their offices, write to them or phone them for more details.

Legal & General   www.landg.com

Being an insurance company, the site has much information on their insurance products. The mortgage section is quite comprehensive. 'Interplan' is a facility to manage a flexible mortgage via the Internet. The main mortgage products include:

- 'Buy to let' mortgages for commercial or domestic letting. This is a variation of their flexible account. It allows for overpayments to cover periods when no rent is coming in, and allows you to buy up to three properties to let.
- 'Equity mover' mortgages – for existing homeowners with little or no equity. This covers mortgages of between 95 and 100 per cent of the valuation. Once the mortgage is less than 95 per cent of the value of the house, you may switch to any other available mortgage from Legal and General.
- 'Welcome' mortgages are for first-time buyers, and include options of cashbacks, discounts, free valuations, etc.
- 'Guaranteed Gold' mortgages offer guarantees on interest rates, no fees up front, no redemption penalties, cashbacks, further advances, and fixed-rate switch facilities.
- 'Flexible Reserve' mortgages allow you to make overpayments, to create an 'available reserve'. This reserve is then available for further borrowing. There is a special version for self-employed people, and a 'drawdown' version with a guaranteed extra borrowing facility. The flexible reserve may be managed by 'Interplan' via the Internet.

This site has many innovative products, and they can be associated with other products (such as insurance) from the same company.

Nationwide Building Society　　　　　　　　www.nationwide.co.uk

Apart from mortgages, this site has some interesting features, including:

- online banking using Microsoft Money 98 and Money 99. You can even order a copy of Money 98 at a discounted price.
- Nationwide football league – all the details of the league tables, for Divisions 1, 2, and 3, and all the fixtures and results for every team in those divisions.
- An index of house prices.

Newcastle Building Society www.newcastle.co.uk

This society offers a wide range of services. The mortgages include a good selection of commercial mortgages, including:

- residential investment
- commercial investment
- industrial units and offices
- doctors' and dentists' surgeries
- accountants' and solicitors' offices
- Registered Social Landlords (otherwise known as housing associations).

Royal Bank of Scotland www.royalbankscot.co.uk

In addition to the other banking services on this site, including direct banking by PC, there is a comprehensive mortgage section. You operate this section by their 'leading questions' button. Simply click on this, and you get a series of 'leading questions', one screen at a time. The first screen asks 'What sort of loan do you require:

- new mortgage or
- raising money from your home?'

You click on your answer, and this leads you to the next screen. Keep answering the questions to get to the next screen, to arrive at the final answer.

This site is one of the few to deal with raising money from your home by releasing the equity in your home.

Teachers Building Society www.teachersbs.co.uk

This society, as the name suggests, started in 1966 for the benefit of teachers. They still lend predominantly to teachers, although the door is not closed to others.

They also specialise in lending to small and medium-sized registered social landlords.

Woolwich plc www.woolwich.co.uk

This is another large organisation, recently demutualised. They offer a wide range of services. Amongst their mortgage products they have:

- Open Plan mortgage. This is a flexible mortgage product combining a mortgage account with bank account facilities.
- Energy Saver mortgage. This combines an orthodox mortgage, with the possibility of fixed rates for limited periods, with incentives in the form of 'energy-efficient domestic appliances' (you can choose one of three packages). There are also ten free energy-saving light bulbs, and free advice from the Energy Saving Trust.
- Direct telephone mortgages – a direct telephone service.
- Direct Buy to Let mortgages – if you wish to buy a property to let.

Mortgage brokers

These are sites run by brokers who do not advertise their own products. They seek to match the right mortgages to your personal circumstances, then find the best products for you, with the best rates available. These are commercial sites. The mortgage brokers earn their living by getting commission for introductions. That does not mean that they are just parasites, though. They have access to a wide range of lenders, and up-to-date information about all the products available. They can get the best deal for you.

Moneynet   www.moneynet.co.uk

This site is owned by Sterling Business Consultants Ltd. It claims independence, and carries advertisements by mortgage lenders. The heart of this site is the search engine, said to be unique. The mortgages search menu first asks you to select one of the four options (see Figure 4). These are:

- Standard – for normal lending on residential property.
- Flexible (or 'lifestyle') mortgages – for mortgages with more flexibility, such as calculation of interest on a daily basis, drawdown facilities, payment breaks, overpayment facilities, etc.
- Impaired credit – for those in arrears with payments, or with county court judgements against them, or 'non-status lending'.
- Buying to let – this searches lenders prepared to lend to people buying a property to let.

After selecting the category, the next page asks for the value of the property, the amount of mortgage required, and the earnings details of you and your spouse or partner. You then choose between the type

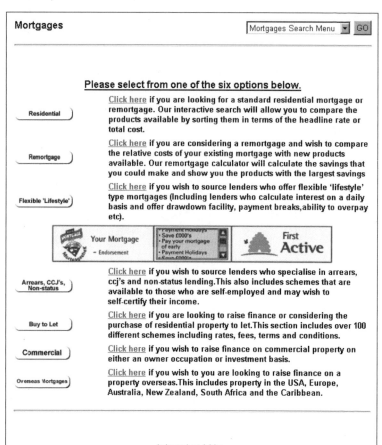

Mortgages

Mortgages Search Menu ▼ GO

Please select from one of the six options below.

Residential

Click here if you are looking for a standard residential mortgage or remortgage. Our interactive search will allow you to compare the products available by sorting them in terms of the headline rate or total cost.

Remortgage

Click here if you are considering a remortgage and wish to compare the relative costs of your existing mortgage with new products available. Our remortgage calculator will calculate the savings that you could make and show you the products with the largest savings

Flexible 'Lifestyle'

Click here if you wish to source lenders who offer flexible 'lifestyle' type mortgages (Including lenders who calculate interest on a daily basis and offer drawdown facility, payment breaks, ability to overpay etc).

Your Mortgage – Endorsement | • Payment Holidays • Save £000's • Pay your mortgage of early • Payment Holidays | First **Active**

Arrears, CCJ's, Non-status

Click here if you wish to source lenders who specialise in arrears, ccj's and non-status lending. This also includes schemes that are available to those who are self-employed and may wish to self-certify their income.

Buy to Let

Click here if you are looking to raise finance or considering the purchase of residential property to let. This section includes over 100 different schemes including rates, fees, terms and conditions.

Commercial

Click here if you wish to raise finance on commercial property on either an owner occupation or investment basis.

Overseas Mortgages

Click here if you wish to you are looking to raise finance on a property overseas. This includes property in the USA, Europe, Australia, New Zealand, South Africa and the Caribbean.

Independent Advice

WARNING:
Whilst every effort is made to ensure that the information published on these pages is accurate, no liability can be accepted for any inaccuracies or any loss suffered as a result. You are advised to discuss the individual circumstances of your particular case with the lender concerned and to confirm the details as they apply in your situation.

On occasions Moneynet may be paid a procuration fee by the lender where business has been transacted.

Fig. 4. Moneynet search facility.

of mortgage (e.g. fixed interest, capped, variable, etc.). The next choice is for interest only repayments, capital and interest, or 'any'. If you are searching on the impaired credit menu, you are then prompted to give an indication of the problem. Submit these details, and the results of the search are then displayed. These results take account of the loan to value ratio and the earnings multiple.

The results are displayed in a table showing:

- the name of the lender
- the interest rate
- the type (e.g. fixed interest, discounted, capped, variable etc.)
- the period of any interest fix or discount
- any fee payable
- the maximum loan to valuation percentage
- any cashback offer
- further notes.

The results are shown in ascending order of the interest rate. However, as their help pages indicate, the lowest rate is not necessarily the best one for you. Always look at the details in the 'notes' column. These details indicate any other conditions, such as early redemption penalties, arrangement fees, or conditional insurance products to qualify.

To make comparisons, you may have to make more than one search. For instance, you may search the discounted interest rates, highlight two or three of the best deals, print them off, then search fixed or variable interest rates, and do the same. You then have printed comparisons.

This site claims to be independent, and the first to provide the information in an interactive way at no cost to the user. They state that every mortgage lender in the UK has been given the opportunity to display their rates on the Moneynet site at no charge, although many lenders have 'banner' type advertisements running through the site. No products are given priority treatment, and no deals will be promoted in preference to a competitive product. They provide a full list of participating lenders on the search page, and are actively seeking further lenders to add.

If you need further advice, you can email a query to Moneynet, who will give further advice, again free of charge. As they are not authorised to sell financial products, they claim to give impartial and unbiased advice.

This is a comprehensive site which should be able to locate a good deal for you.

1st People's Mortgage   www.first.co.uk

This site is the property of 1st People's Mortgage Ltd. of Bristol, a broker offering a wide range of products, including:

- county court judgements and cleared bankruptcies
- mortgage arrears
- right to buy in excess of purchase price
- enhanced income multiples
- remortgages a speciality
- self-employed a speciality
- pay off those expensive credit card balances
- repay expensive personal loans
- self-certification up to 90 per cent
- properties for letting
- holiday homes
- accelerated mortgages.

The Mortgage Guild   www.theguild.co.uk

This site is owned by The Mortgage Guild, a firm of brokers in Braintree. It offers various options including self-employed and impaired-credit lending. It also offers free software to analyse and assess your own mortgage. It claims to enable you to change payment structures to see if you could save money. It also offers a free money-saving guide. The boast is 'We are confident that everyone who reads it can change something about their mortgage that will bring about a saving'.

There is also a free draw on this site.

UK Mortgage Brokers   www.mortgagebroker.co.uk

This broker offers the usual mix of fixed rates, discounts, capped rates, cashbacks, etc. One useful feature is the section on 100 per cent mortgages. It also has a section for IT professionals

Yellow Brick Road   www.yellowbrickroad.co.uk

This is a broker firm which specialises in impaired credit lending. Their claim is that they will take a fresh look at your application. The web site only has three pages, all of which are very brief. The pages are:

- who we are
- the promise
- application.

They do not promise to say 'yes', but they do give six promises:

1. We promise to listen.
2. We promise to try.
3. We promise to be honest.
4. We promise to be responsible.
5. We promise to be competitive.
6. We promise to deal direct.

The application is simply an information form for you to fill in your details and send to them.

This site is brief and to the point, and if you have problems getting a mortgage it could well come up with what you need.

Instant Mortgage Centre	www.loans4u.co.uk

This is another broker dealing with impaired credit lending, but also more. Their emphasis is on people having difficulty getting a mortgage, for whatever reason. The reasons could include:

- being self-employed
- employed with no proof of income
- not having a bank account
- having a county court judgement or being in arrears
- wanting to buy a council home
- remortgages
- buying to let.

The service is available to UK citizens only. Apart from the home page, the web site only consists of an application form. All dealing thereafter is direct with the company.

Elite Mortgages	www.elitemortgages.co.uk

As the name suggests, this is a more upmarket company. They are not interested in impaired credit lending, and discourage applicants with these sort of problems. Their range of activities include:

- commercial mortgages
- commercial refinance
- residential mortgages
- remortgages
- purchase of property overseas
- foreign nationals purchasing property in the UK
- buying property to let.

This site is owned by Elite Mortgages Ltd, a firm of mortgage brokers.

Mortgages Online   www.mortgages-online.co.uk

This is the site of an Internet-based firm of independent financial advisers called IFA-Online Ltd. They have sites devoted to mortgages online, pensions online, and investments online.

The site has a 'best buys' page which is updated twice daily, giving news of the best deals around. They also know who can offer you 100 per cent mortgages, and offer a 'Mortgages-online maximum loan certificate'.

There is also a mortgage calculator, and an online guide for first-time buyers. Needless to say, there is also an application form to email to them.

Other services
If you want to buy or sell your home through the Internet, there are several sites you can access. Most have pictures of properties for sale, and allow you to search by location, price range and number of bedrooms.

Find a Property	www.findaproperty.com
Homepages	www. homepages.co.uk
Homes On-Line UK	www.homes-on-line.com
Hot Property	www. hot-property.com
Houseweb	www.houseweb.co.uk

Home to Home   www.home-to-home.co.uk

This is an Internet magazine for those buying or selling a house, and there are sections for advertising your home, mortgages, etc.

Property World   www.propertyworld.co.uk

UpMyStreet   www.upmystreet.com

This site gives you useful information about the area you are searching, including such things as crime rates, property prices, council tax
and ambulance response times. These figures are also shown as
comparisons with the national averages.

CHECKLIST

1. Decide how much you can afford.

2. Find the right house.

3. Decide on the repayment method.

4. Make sure you get adequate insurance cover.

5. Look for the best deal.

6. Search the lenders direct, or try the brokers' sites.

5

Banking Online

Running your bank account from your PC is now possible. It gives you the advantage of virtually unlimited access – most services are available for most of the 24 hours each day.

Security is always a concern, and providers give full encryption security, together with password protection. Lloyds Online, for example, asks for a user ID, which is in the form of a six digit figure, like bank sorting codes, and a password. First Direct asks for the 1st, 3rd and last letters of the password. Online banking is considered at least as secure as telephone banking.

Many banks, including Barclays, Lloyds TSB and Citibank, offer a free Internet service as an incentive to join their online banking.

WEB SITES

Barclays Bank   www.barclays.co.uk

The free Internet service for customers of Barclays is available at www.is.barclays.net. The online service also has an extensive demonstration site.

The bank uses the site to promote its other services, including insurances, share dealing, mortgages, and so on.

The personal services and products have the following web site address: www.personal.barclays.co.uk. This gives you access to all the available services, including current and savings accounts, insurance, loans, mortgages, telephone and online banking, travel services, making a will, and special services for young people and students.

Citibank   www.citibank.com

This is available 24 hours a day. Security is featured very highly on this site. There are three levels of encryption:

1. strong encryption

2. direct access with an ID number

3. auto time-out – this means that after four minutes of inactivity, it closes down. The online demonstration is a little sparse, showing the bare minimum.

Co-operative Bank   https://the.co-operativebank.co.uk

This site also has an Internet banking demonstration, although it can take several minutes to download.

The site gives a high profile to the bank's much publicised ethical stance. One section, for example, deals with 'Bringing the Arms Trade into the Open'. There is also a section for 'Customers who Care' and who can put their care into action by using the bank's card.

Coutts and Co   www.coutts.com

This bank has a proud history as an independent, rather exclusive banker. Now it is the private arm of NatWest bank. It offers many services, including:

- investment management
- art advisory service
- retirement service
- tax advice and planning
- estate and inheritance planning
- education services
- services to professionals
- services for business owners
- financial planning
- residential property services
- commercial banking services
- banking and credit services.

Egg   www.egg.com

This is the Internet banking arm of the Prudential Plc. It is unusual in offering an Internet-only savings account, giving a rate of interest which is usually better than most other accounts. It also offers mortgages, loans, savings accounts, and an investment supermarket. It promotes its credit card, and uses its web site to encourage you to use the card – with suggestions for things like Christmas shopping. (See Figure 5.)

First Direct   www.firstdirect.co.uk

This is the Internet banking arm of HSBC (formerly called Midland Bank). First Direct offers 24-hour online banking. The web site gives a comprehensive demonstration. You may carry out all the normal banking operations, and view balances on all accounts with them. You may also view transactions for up to 100 days on each account and print the transactions or download them to use in programs on your PC such as Microsoft Money, Intuit, Quicken, or your own spreadsheet.

You can register to open an account, or simply to receive more information.

First-e   www.first-e.com

This is the Internet trading name of the French bank Banque d'Escompte. However, its British incarnation is thoroughly British. It offers a current account, a savings account and an investment account. Interest rates are competitive on the savings account, and the current account operates on a 'no charges' basis.

It strongly promotes the IPO option (Initial Public Offering), which gives the bank's customers access to first-time flotations of new and young companies, for investment purposes.

First Trust Bank   www.ftbni.co.uk

This is an Irish bank with headquarters in Belfast.

HSBC   www.banking.hsbc.co.uk

This is the bank formerly called Midland Bank, and no doubt many people will continue to call it that for some time to come. On offer are the usual full range of current accounts, savings accounts, credit and debit cards, and loans. There is also the option of TV banking.

Fig. 5. Egg home page.

Lloyds TSB Bank www.lloydstsb.co.uk

Lloyds Bank offers a full online banking service for personal customers and sole traders. There is a demonstration online. Other banking products and services include:

- savings accounts
- Budget account
- Classic account
- debit and credit cards

- Gold Service account
- telephone banking
- student accounts
- young saver's account.

Nationwide Building Society	www.nationwide.co.uk

This is the biggest remaining building society, and it promotes an online banking service. There is a demonstration mode, and you can get applications for current accounts, savings, loans, mortgages, credit cards online. There is also a secure message facility.

NatWest Bank	www.natwest.co.uk

NatWest promote themselves as 'more than just a bank'. They claim to be the leader in banking for small businesses and new businesses. Their web site includes details of 24-hour PC banking. There are interactive features including a currency converter, a mortgage calculator, instant quotes for travel insurance, a personal loan calculator, a young person's cash calculator, a competition and games.

Royal Bank of Scotland	www.royalbankscot.co.uk

This bank offers a wide range of banking facilities, with PC banking on the Internet available for businesses.

Standard Chartered Bank	www.stanchart.com

This bank has its roots in Hong Kong, and is strongest in its Asian and Chinese connections.

Standard Life Bank	www.standardlifebank.com

This bank is part of the Standard Life group, which is mainly a pensions and life assurance company. However, it started its banking arm in 1998, and has attracted a large amount of money into its accounts – particularly savings accounts, with good rates of interest.

Triodos Bank	www.triodos.co.uk

This is one of Europe's leading ethical banks. It started life in Holland, but has a thriving UK branch. It specialises in financing initiatives giving social or environmental benefits. The web site gives details of its saving and investing accounts, personal banking, business banking and charity banking.

Virgin Direct	www.virgin-direct.co.uk

This company offers banking and investments on the web site. It proudly champions the concept of tracker funds, which it claims to have pioneered. The accounts it offers are the deposit account and the 'one' account, which combines a mortgage with a current account.

6

Planning your Pension on the Internet

Your retirement is the longest holiday you will ever take. Make sure that you provide adequately to enjoy that holiday. The basic state pension does not really give an adequate income for most people's expectations. The government provides incentives by way of tax relief to encourage people to save for their retirement.

Probably the best advice is to start saving for your retirement as early as you can. You are never too young. This theme is taken up by the many sites dealing with pensions. They nearly all emphasise that you should do it as soon as possible. Of course, they are trying to sell their products, but in this case, the advice is sound.

Make sure you understand the various elements that make up the pension you get when you retire. These include:

- state pension
- stakeholder pensions
- superannuation schemes, provided by employers
- additional voluntary contributions to an employer's scheme
- personal pension schemes, for employed or self-employed people.

For each of these, you need to know:

- how you qualify
- what you may contribute
- the way the benefits are worked out.

Stakeholder pensions are still in the preparation stage, and will be introduced in April 2001. They are to be aimed at the 8.5 million people estimated by the government to be in employment or self-employment, and not making any pension provision. They are to be low cost, flexible pension plans. Many of the web sites give information about stakeholder pensions. If you are starting a new pension plan, make sure it enables you to switch to a stakeholder pension at the right time if necessary.

REGULATORY BODIES

If you have any problem, you should, of course, try to sort it out with your pension provider. However, there are a number of regulatory bodies which can help with difficulties.

The Pensions Advisory Service   www.opas.org.uk

This site gives you a clear explanation of their powers in resolving disputes, and you can email them through the web site.

The Occupational Pensions Regulatory Authority   www.opra.gov.uk

This body regulates company pensions, making sure that the funds are properly run, and the funds properly invested. It has a pension tracing service, which may help if you have lost track of a company pension.

The National Association of Pension Funds   www.napf.co.uk

This organisation helps those running occupational pension schemes. It provides information on legislation which may affect your scheme.

TAKING THE BENEFITS

The state pension is provided by:

Department for Social Security   www.dss.gov.uk

There is a direct link to the Benefits Agency from the home page of the DSS site. The Benefits Agency gives information on all the benefits available. From here, you can click directly on to a section telling you how to get a pension forecast. If you are more than four months away from qualifying for your pension, you can get a forecast of what your pension will be. You have to get form BR 19, which you can download from the site. However, you cannot transmit it by Internet. You have to complete it and send it by snail mail to the DSS headquarters in Newcastle.

The home page of the DSS provides a link to the War Pensions Agency, which is a separate department from the Benefits Agency. This gives you information about war pensions.

The home page also highlights 'Impartial Information about

Pensions'. This is a series of eight leaflets to help you make an informed decision about your pension and retirement. These are truly impartial, and give you a good background to the whole subject. They are well worth reading if you are going to invest seriously in a pension fund.

Taking benefits from private schemes

There are also several ways to take the benefits from private pension schemes. Amongst the decisions you might have to make are:

- Should I take the Open Market Option? The pension fund you have built up can be used by you to take a pension from any provider – not just the company with which you built up the pension fund. The difference between the best and the worst pension annuity rates on offer can be quite considerable, especially if you have a large amount in your pension fund.

- Should I take the tax free lump sum, with a reduced pension, or should I take the full pension?

- Can I benefit from phased retirement? This is particularly useful if you want to retire gradually, by cutting down progressively on your working days.

- Should I think about the drawdown option? This means that you can draw down a percentage of the capital sum each year (until you reach a certain age). This is beneficial when the annuity rates are low, since otherwise you would have to lock yourself into a permanently low annuity rate for the rest of your life.

- On what basis should I take the pension annuity? There are several ways to take this, including
  - a fixed amount
  - a pension escalating at a fixed percentage rate each year
  - a pension which increases by matching the rate of inflation each year
  - a pension on the joint lives of yourself and your spouse.

In view of the many choices available, it may be a good idea to consult an Independent Financial Adviser. You can, of course, find one on the Internet.

WEB SITES – PENSION PROVIDERS

There are many companies in the business of providing pension funds. Most of these provide a showcase for their products on the Internet. Here are some of them.

CIS Pensions   www.cis.co.uk

This is the Co-operative Insurance Society. It claims over one million personal pension policies in force, making it one of the top ten providers in the UK. The pensions section of the site is simple and straightforward.

Clerical Medical   www.clericalmedical.co.uk

This company offers a Personal Pension Plan, a Free Standing Additional Voluntary Contribution Plan and a Retirement Selection Plan. There is also a useful guide to life in retirement.

Direct Line   www.directline.com

This is the direct 'phone insurance company which advertises on the television with the red telephone. Their pensions products are limited, but flexible. The web site emphasises that there are only two funds, and only two low charges.

There are no penalties for stopping contributions, decreasing them, retiring early or transferring out. This means that it copes with the real world, where people move house, get ill, change jobs, have kids, etc. That is flexibility.

The product summary gives a concise guide to the main features of the pension products.

Equitable Life   www.equitable.co.uk

This is one of the biggest mutual companies, and one of the oldest. It was founded in 1762. The site includes details of its pension plans, as well as its other products.

Fleming Investment Trusts   www.flemings.co.uk

This is an investment trust company, but it does have two pension accounts – one for the employed and one for the self-employed. The site gives an outline of these plans, and an investor's guide, which can be downloaded.

Gartmore   www.gartmore.iii.co.uk

This company offers a Personal Pension Trust, which is a unit trust scheme with a range of 16 funds. There are mixed funds, equity funds, bond funds and a deposit fund. Under their LifePlan, you can restructure the funds as you progress through your working life. There is a high exposure to equity funds for younger people, progressively switching to more secure bonds and deposits as retirement approaches.

Legal & General   www.landg.com

This large company gives details of its pension plans, and has much information about stakeholder pensions. In particular, it gives a checklist to ensure that your pension is 'stakeholder friendly' (see Figure 6).

Legal & General guarantees that for all Personal Pension Plans taken out now, if you transfer to a Legal & General Stakeholder pension, the transferred fund will be worth at least as much as if you had bought a Legal & General Stakeholder pension from the time you took out the Personal Pension Plan.

Marks and Spencer
Financial Services   www. marks-and-spencer.co.uk/financial-services

This is another retailer which has moved into financial services. The pensions section emphasises the low charges, because they do not pay commission. You can click on further pages to get detailed information about the plans, and contact the company, directly, online or by telephone.

National Mutual   www.nationalmutual.co.uk

This is a mutual insurance company (i.e. it is owned by its members, not shareholders). The site warns you quite clearly that they only do business through independent advisers, so you cannot deal directly with them. However, they give a list of advisers so that you can choose one near you.

Fig. 6. Legal & General pensions home page.

Norwich Union   www.norwich-union.co.uk

Amongst its many investment and insurance products, Norwich Union offers pensions. The web site gives a summary of what pensions are, and details of its products. It emphasises, however, that you should seek professional financial advice, and there is a link to find a professional adviser.

Royal Liver Assurance   www.royal-liver.com

This is a registered Friendly Society, which gives it certain tax advantages. The pensions section of the site is straightforward, with no frills.

Scottish Widows   www.scottishwidows.co.uk

This is an elegant looking site, featuring the attractive woman from the newspaper and television adverts. It highlights their products, which include more than just pensions. Clicking on the 'Products' bar allows you to survey the company's products and you can also download application forms. The pension centre (see Figure 7) emphasises the effects of inflation, and pushes home the message 'start now'. It explains personal pensions, stakeholder pensions, SERPs, life cover and payment protection.

Standard Life   www.standardlife.co.uk

This is another mutual company, and one of the biggest. It boasts that it is one of only two UK life companies to be given the top 'Triple A' rating by Standard and Poors, the independent rating agency.

The site gives brief details of the various types of pension products available and, of course, the opportunity to contact the company.

Sun Life   www.axaequityandlaw.co.uk

This is a large company, a member of the Axa group. Its pension products are shown on the site, and the company sponsors the FA Cup, so there is also much information about football.

Sun Life of Canada   www.slocpensions.co.uk

A simple and straightforward site, it gives you access to the worldwide site of SLOC.

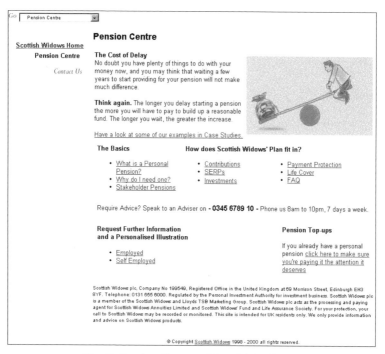

Fig. 7. Pension Centre of Scottish Widows.

Teachers Group   www.teachers-group.co.uk

As the name suggests, this company is tailored for teachers. Pensions is one area which they cover. The site includes useful information about public sector occupational pensions, and helps you to plan and maximise your benefits in retirement.

Tesco Personal Finance   www.tesco.co.uk

Tesco has recently come into the personal finance market. Their pensions products are the result of a joint venture with Scottish Widows. They emphasise their 'transparency' in their 'pension promise':

- They won't sell you a pension that's not right for you.
- If they don't have a pension that's right for you, they will tell you right away.
- No hidden charges.
- You can have as much or as little pension advice as you want.

- You can start stop, increase or decrease your payments without penalty.
- You can start from as little as £1 per day.

Virgin Direct   www.virgin-direct.co.uk

The pensions section is part of the Virgin Direct financial web site. This gives a simple guide to personal pensions, whether you are employed or self-employed. The 'start saving now' message is hammered home, and you can contact the company to make an application.

USING ADVISERS

You could also get advice from brokers or Independent Financial Advisers. They are intermediaries, who will look around for the best pension for you, in return for a commission. They will also advise you about the best way of taking the benefits, when the time comes. Some advisers may be happy to charge you a flat fee instead of taking commission, and some take a reduced commission, such as:

Discount Pensions   www.discountpensions.co.uk

This is a firm which does its business over the Internet, and claims to be able to reduce its costs dramatically. It is therefore able to reduce its commission to 1 per cent plus an administrative fee of £25. This means more of the premium you pay goes into the pension fund, and you therefore get a better pension at the end.

If the adviser takes a reduced commission, they inform the insurance or pension company, so that your pension fund gets credited with a little extra – the amount of commission they would normally have paid, but which is given up.

Independent Financial Advisers Association   www.ifaa.org.uk

This is the body which regulates Independent Financial Advisers. If you have any queries or complaints, this is the first stop.

IFA Promotion Ltd   www.unbiased.co.uk

This is an organisation which promotes Independent Financial Advisers. They will send you the names of three local IFAs, and a voucher for a free 'no obligation' consultation.

Financial Information Network Directory   www.find.co.uk/advice/AIFA.html

---

This address takes you straight to the page on FIND which lists the Independent Financial Advisers. There are well over three hundred listed, so you have no lack of choice. As you will see, some of them deal specially with pensions.

CHECKLIST

1. Make sure you provide adequately to enjoy your retirement.

2. Get a pension forecast from the Benefits Agency.

3. Look for the pension which suits your circumstances.

4. Get advice from an IFA if you are unsure, or feel that the issues are too complex.

7

Getting Insurance on the Internet

KNOWING WHAT TO LOOK OUT FOR

Many insurance companies are large concerns which have branched out into other fields such as banking and pensions. In return, banks and building societies have come into insurance.

When looking for insurance on the net, remember always the golden rule – **they are trying to sell to you**. Their web sites are their shop window. Take time to look carefully at what they are offering. One company may appear to be offering a cheaper premium, but are you really comparing like with like?

Another thing to bear in mind when looking for insurance on the net is: are you looking at the site of an insurance company (i.e. a provider of insurance) or a broker? A broker is an agent who earns commission from insurance companies by selling their insurance. However, to earn that commission, he has to be of service to you. He provides that service by comparing costs for an insurance policy, and comparing the terms of the insurance.

Here are some key questions to ask when trying to compare insurance quotes:

- Are there any no claim bonuses – and if so, how much?
- Can I protect the no claims bonus?
- Can I get a quote online?
- Can I pay the premium online?
- What are the claims procedures? Is there, for instance, a 24-hour telephone helpline?
- Can I pay premiums monthly – and if so, does it cost extra?

INSURANCE COMPANIES

Here are some sites of insurance companies offering general insurance.

Axa www.axa-insurance.co.uk

This site has a lot of sports coverage. The Axa sponsorship of the FA cup means that they give much space to football. Cricket, rugby league, rugby union, boxing, golf, tennis and motor sports also figure highly here, and you can get Sky sports coverage. Oh, and yes, it does say something about their insurance products. They have policies to cover homes, weddings, mechanical breakdown, the licensed trade, motors (private and commercial), personal accident and commercial insurance

Boots Insurance www.boots.co.uk

This is the retail chemist, who also offer travel insurance and health insurance.

CGU www.cgu-direct.co.uk

You can get information, including online quotes, for various types of insurance, including motor, home (contents and buildings) and travel.

Churchill www.churchill.co.uk

This company is a relatively new one, having been founded in 1989. It does not deal with many products outside of insurance. Apart from the usual insurance products you would expect – car insurance, home insurance, pet insurance, travel insurance, etc. – it also offers credit cards and loans.

The site is straightforward, and the cute bulldog cartoon appears on every page. He is also available as a screen saver (see Figure 8).

CIS Co-operative Insurance www.cis.co.uk

This is the only co-operative insurance company, and offers motor and home insurance, with instant illustrations of premiums, and a prize draw which you enter by telling them the renewal date of your present insurance. They also do life assurance and pensions, mortgages and a unit trust.

They also host the web site for Blackburn Rovers football club.

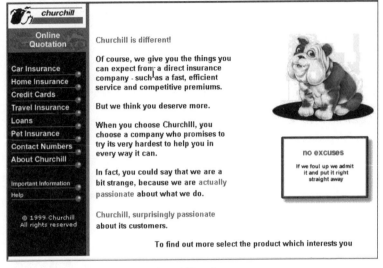

Fig. 8. Churchill welcome page.

Cornhill   www.cornhill.co.uk

The insurance details on this site include:

- personal – motor, home, life, travel, pets, musical instruments, and weddings
- commercial – business products, commercial motors, Drivecare, engineering, and risk management.

They sponsor test cricket at present, although that will shortly cease. The site currently has a large section devoted to cricket, with fixtures, links and computer games.

Direct Line   www.directline.com

This is the company which advertises on television, and was one of the forerunners in telephone insurance companies. You can get quotes via the site. Its products now include motor, pet, travel and home insurance, a rescue service for motorists, mortgages and loans, savings, a credit card, life assurance and pensions, and ISAs.

You can click on the chameleon for 'fun'. This takes you into a section of arcade type games featuring the red telephone we all know (and love?) from the television adverts (see Figure 9).

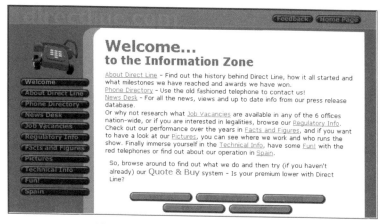

Fig. 9. Direct Line information zone.

Eagle Star   www.eaglestardirect.co.uk

You will find the usual information about insurances, including home, motor, travel and boat insurance.

Ecclesiastical Insurance Group   www.eigonline.co.uk

As the name suggests, this group was originally created to insure churches. However, it now has a wide range of products. They include home insurance, motor insurance, savings and investments, commercial and industrial insurance, wedding insurance, and legal expenses insurance. Other 'goodies' on the site include a group purchasing scheme to save you money on many items, education benefits, and special needs of charities and their workers.

Legal & General   www.landg.com

This is one of the giants of the insurance industry. The web site is extensive and sophisticated; their involvement in other services is dealt with in the relevant chapters. As to general insurance, they deal in home insurance and health care.

The web site gimmick is the 'Umbrella club'.

NFU Mutual   www.nfumutual.co.uk

This is a mutual company operated by the National Farmers Union. As you would expect, it has specialist insurance products for farmers, and an insurance for horses and ponies. It also deals in general commercial insurance, travel, motor, home and contents, and life assurance and pensions.

Norwich Union   www.norwich-union.co.uk

This large insurance company offers many products, including investments and pensions, as well as its more general insurances. The general insurances include:

- life assurance
- motor insurance
- motor cycle insurance
- home insurance
- household appliances insurance
- mortgage cover.

Pearl   www.pearl.co.uk

The home page of this site emphasises 'Personal Welfare'. The buttons to click are:

- Personal welfare.
- How can Pearl help you?
- Pearl's commitment to you.

Trying to get any information can be frustrating – all the site does is give you contacts to find out more about the company and its products.

Prudential   www.pru.co.uk

They are probably best known for life assurance and pensions, but they also deal with motor and home insurance.

Royal Liver Assurance   www.royal-liver.com

This is a well laid out site, the 'virtual shop' showing a clear summary of the company's products. These include savings and investments, serious illness insurance, pensions, life assurance, mortgages, home insurance and motor insurance.

Their 'gimmicks' include selections from the *Guinness Book of Records* entitled 'Strange Lives' – a selection of oddities, such as the man who was a midget until the age of 21, but was over seven feet tall when he died. They also have a millennium section and a competition – which is really a free draw for those who send for a quote.

Royal London Insurance   www. royal-london-insurance.co.uk

Not much by way of fireworks on this site, but a no-nonsense guide to the way insurance (and in particular their insurance) can help you through the financial maze.

Saga   www.saga.co.uk/sagaservices/

This is the company for over-50s only. As well as its travel agent and its magazine, it deals with insurance for members – home, motor, motor breakdown, caravan, private medical, personal accident, pet and travel insurance.

Tesco Personal Finance   www.tesco.co.uk

This, of course, is the retail giant's financial services arm. Among other things, it offers motor, home, pet and travel insurance.

Teachers Group   www.teachers-group.co.uk

This company deals mainly with teachers. Its general insurance products include home and motor insurance. Other products include pensions, life insurance, savings and investments, loans and credit cards, and a travel club.

BANKS AND BUILDING SOCIETIES

Barclays Bank   www.personal.barclays.co.uk

This bank offers travel, student, home, personal accident and motor cover.

HSBC Insurance Brokers	www.hsbcgibbs.com

This is a more specialist insurance broking company. It promotes itself as 'the market leader in supplying specialist insurance services to individuals and companies whose needs extend beyond the scope of direct insurers'. They deal in insurances for the home, personal health, marine, jewellery, estates, schools and reinsurance.

Lambeth Building Society	www.simplydirect.co.uk

This is the telephone response arm of the Lambeth Building Society, offering motor, home, travel, life assurance and a home buyers and sellers cost insurance.

Lloyds TSB Bank	www.lloydstsb.co.uk

This bank has a range of insurances covering accident protection, asset payment protection, buildings, health cover, loan protection, home contents, mortgage protection, personal overdraft protection, and travel insurance.

SPECIALIST INSURANCE COMPANIES

Some companies are true specialists. They concentrate on one type of insurance only – and hope to attract customers by their specialist knowledge.

Health insurance

This really means private medical insurance, to cover hospital and medical expenses not provided by the National Health Service. Most people have heard of BUPA and Private Patients' Plan, but there are over 30 medical insurers offering private schemes.

BUPA	www.bupa.co.uk

This is the biggest health care insurance company in this country. Its web site offers latest health news, topical tips, such as fireworks safety tips, and air miles offers. They offer business plans for employers, and as well as health care, they offer travel insurance and critical illness cover. The web site also has a locator to find 'the nearest one to you', covering private hospitals and other types of health establishments.

CS Healthcare   www.cshealthcare.co.uk

This company specialises in providing health insurance for present and former civil servants, employees in the public sector, and privatised industries. It is a non-profit-making Friendly Society.

Exeter Friendly Society   www.exeterfriendly.co.uk

This society advertises the fact that it provides private medical insurance which doesn't raise your premiums simply because you get older.

Hospital Savings Association   www.hsahealthcare.org

This is a non-profit organisation, and is best known for the savings plans for cash benefits for treatment for medical, dental, optical treatment, etc.

Medibroker   www.medibroker.com

As the name suggests, this is a firm of insurance brokers specialising in medical insurance. They are further specialised in that they are run for, and by, expatriates. They advise on many areas, including:

- private medical insurance worldwide
- income protection plans
- critical illness plans
- emergency plans only
- personal accident plans
- extended travel options
- dental and maternity options
- plans in sterling or US dollars
- mortal remains recovery
- term life cover
- group or company plans.

There are also useful links from this site.

Medicus   www.medicus.co.uk

This company offers cover in the UK and abroad.

Prime Health   www.primehealth.co.uk

This is a wholly owned subsidiary of Standard Life, the large mutual insurance group.

Private Health Associates   www. phahealth.co.uk

This is a firm of UK and international brokers, dealing in cover for:

- medical insurance
- long-term care
- critical illness
- income protection
- expatriate medical insurance
- pet insurance
- travel insurance
- financial advice.

The Private Health Partnership   www.php.co.uk

This is an independent consultancy providing impartial advice on a full range of medical and dental insurance schemes.

Private Patients' Plan   www.ppphealthcare.co.uk

The second largest company in this field after BUPA, this company offers a wide range of health insurances.

Western Provident Association   www.wpahealth.co.uk

This is another large company, insuring over 500,000 people, and over 5,000 companies. It claims a high degree of value for money and independence, being a non-profit provident company, which does not own or run any hospitals.

William Russell   www.william-russell.co.uk

This company specialises in health care protection for people living or travelling overseas.

Building trades insurance

B&CE Insurance   www.bandce.co.uk

'B and CE' stands for 'building and civil engineering'. This site offers low cost personal insurance policies for individuals in the construction industry. Their products include 'RapidCash' accident insurance, compulsory purchase annuity and life assurance.

Legal protection insurance

DAS   www.das.co.uk

This company specialises in legal protection cover. It was mainly known for motor legal protection, but it now also covers marine, family, consumer disputes and commercial legal protection. The web site gives help on accident management, legal advice, assistance and counselling.

Motor insurance

Admiral   www.admiral.co.uk

This company specialises in motor insurance. It offers you a 10 per cent discount for using the quote line to get a telephone quote.

Dial Direct Insurance   www.ddirect.co.uk

This company offers cover for motor cars and motor cycles. The cover includes:

- third party cover while driving other vehicles
- instalments scheme
- 24-hour windscreen service
- repairer network
- free courtesy car.

Eclipse Insurance   www.eclipse-insurance.co.uk

This is a Lloyds broker specialising in motor insurance. They provide cover for:

- protected no claims bonus

- windscreen cover
- personal effects
- audio equipment
- personal accident
- medical expenses.

Serviceline (UK) Ltd   www.serviceline.co.uk

This company claims value for money, with several features as standard:

- free 90-day foreign use cover
- 24-hour helpline facilities
- damage to third party property cover
- unlimited cover for injuries to third parties
- fast and effective claim service
- free anti-theft etching service.

Optional extras include:

- instalment facilities to spread the cost of premiums
- up to £25,000 legal expenses cover
- protected no claim bonus
- cover for in-car entertainment over £750
- personal accident cover for drivers
- new for old cover.

Pet insurance

Look out for sites which offer information about your pets, some veterinary questions, tips of the month, and such things as a reminder service via email for things like vaccinations, etc.

Healthy Pets   www.healthy-pets.co.uk

This is an independent intermediary specialising in pet insurance.

Pet Healthcare Insurance   www.pethealthcareinsurance.co.uk

This site has much information about looking after dogs and cats, a tip of the month, an email reminder service and an offer of free insurance for one month. The insurance is underwritten by Royal and Sun Alliance.

PETline	http://195.173.143.146/NetPet

This is an independent broker which specialises in animal insurance.

Pet Plan	www.petplan.co.uk

This company is backed by Cornhill insurance. The web site offers information about animals, veterinary matters and, of course, their insurance policies.

Petshield	www.petproducts.co.uk

This company offers insurance for dogs and cats, covering the following risks:

- illness and accident
- early death
- loss by theft or straying
- behavioural problems
- accidental damage
- third party claims
- boarding fees
- advertising and rewards.

There is a 15 per cent surcharge for certain breeds of dog.

Scottish Pet Insurance	www.scotpet.co.uk

This insurer specialises in insurance of dogs and cats. You can apply and pay online. It has sections for animal questions, and a vet area.

Travel insurance
If you want to gaze at alluring pictures of exotic-looking places, you will find plenty in the travel insurance sites.

Assured Travel Insurance	www.britsurf.org/dial-direct/assured.html

This company provides a Travel Bond, annual multi-trip insurance, the Varsity Bond and Varsity Bond Plus (for young independent travellers), ski and winter sports cover, and Green Flag European Vehicle Breakdown Assistance. They also offer travel insurance for those starting the journey outside the UK or Eire, and a health care insurance for expatriates.

Atlas Travel Insurance	www.travel-insurance.co.uk

Atlas Travel boasts a wide range of policies, including activity cover, and a 'world class computer system'. They also provide a number of humorous stories from their claims department.

Club Direct	www.clubdirect.co.uk

This company emphasises its flexibility. It offers a range of standard policies, but these can be designed for travellers with special needs. Its standard policies cover:

- single trip
- annual multi-trip
- backpackers and long-term travellers
- winter sports
- Continental motoring breakdown
- USA or Canada car rental insurance.

Columbus Direct	www.columbusdirect.co.uk

The usual travel insurance facilities for single-trip or annual policies are on offer at this site. It also has a section giving travel tips and the latest news about various locations in the world that may be dangerous, or need special note, for travellers.

Down Under Insurance	www.downunderinsurance.co.uk

Despite its name, it covers worldwide travel, not just to Australia and New Zealand. This company provides backpacker cover, a comprehensive policy, and adventure travel insurance, which covers you for things like safaris, horse riding, bungee jumping, scuba diving, motor cycling, white water rafting and surfing.

Nomad Insurance	www.nomad-insurance.co.uk

This company offers you a 'free gift' when you take out one of their insurances. There is information aplenty on the site about various travel destinations, and a competition. There is a section with travelling hints to make your trip a happier, safer and claim-free experience. You can also email your travel tips to share on the web site. The best ones published qualify for a free gift.

PHA	www.demon.co.uk/dayco/phamainx.html

This company offers:

- trip cover
- young travellers' cover (up to 35)
- over 65s cover
- long stay cover
- winter sports cover
- annual policies.

Travel Insurance Club	www.travelinsuranceclub.co.uk

This provides travel insurance policies underwritten at Lloyds. It provides backpackers insurance – for the younger worldwide traveller – and short-trip insurance to cover business or holiday travel from five days to two months.

Under The Sun	www.underthesun.co.uk

This company offers policies underwritten by CNA and Royal & Sun Alliance.

WorldCover Direct	www.worldcover.com

Specialist in travel insurance, with a comprehensive annual travel package.

Worldtrekker Travel Insurance	www.worldtrekker.com

This company offers independent travellers value-for-money insurance. It is available to UK residents, and Australian, New Zealand or South African citizens temporarily in the UK.

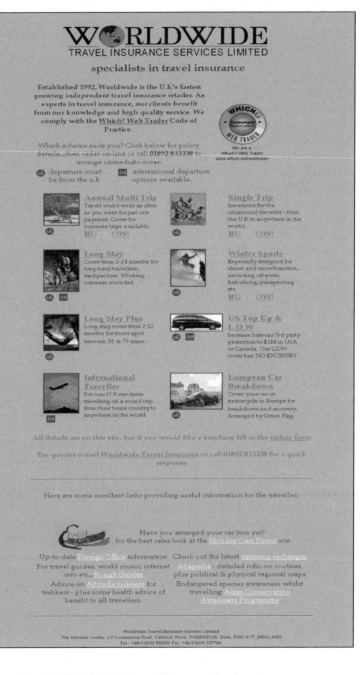

Fig. 10. World Wide Travel Insurance Services home page.

Worldwide Travel Insurance Services Ltd   www.wwtis.co.uk

This company belongs to the Which? Web Trader Code of Practice. It offers:

- annual multi-trip policies
- single-trip policies
- long-stay policies
- international traveller cover for journeys starting outside the UK
- winter sports cover
- US top-up cover
- European car breakdown cover.

You can get an online quote and pay online (see Figure 10).

USING BROKERS AND INDEPENDENT INTERMEDIARIES

These search for the best policies amongst the companies with whom they deal. Look out for the range of companies they deal with, and ask – are there any significant gaps?

Auto Direct   www.yell.co.uk/sites/autodirect

Motor insurance specialists.

The Automobile Association UK   www.theaa.co.uk

This is, of course, the motoring organisation which provides breakdown cover and motoring and travel services. However, AA Insurance Services is the largest personal insurance intermediary in the country (see Figure 11).

Bell Direct   www.belldirect.co.uk

Motor insurance specialist.

Car Insurance Centre   www. carsource.co.uk

Motor insurance specialist.

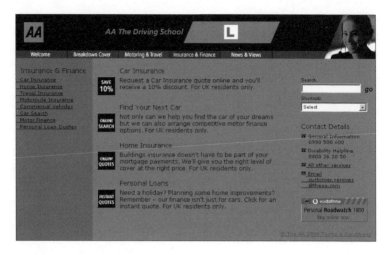

Fig. 11. The Automobile Association insurance and finance page.

Firebond Insurance   www.firebond.co.uk

Motor insurance specialist. They have special quotes for classic cars, Land Rovers and other specialist areas, such as Northern Ireland, wedding cars, etc.

First National Motor Finance   www.firstnationalmotorfinance.co.uk

---

As the name suggests, this company deals mainly in finance for buying cars. However, it does also provide insurance for motoring, and for protection on loan repayments.

Intersure   www.intersure.co.uk

Motor, home, travel, and wedding insurance. A fee-based intermediary. They do not accept commission from the insurance companies.

Motor Insurance Experts   www.insurance-experts.co.uk

Although the name suggests they specialise in motor insurance, they do also cover home and travel insurance. They are a national firm of brokers offering competitive quotes on 90 per cent of the schemes available in the UK.

RHN Riley Insurances Ltd　　http://freespace.virgin.net/rileys.insurance

This company gives a free offer – 12 months' legal protection cover with every new motor or home insurance policy taken out.

Screentrade　　　　　　　　　　　　www.screentrade.co.uk

This is an Internet company which does some comparisons for you. You can compare prices and policies, and their boast is that you can reduce your premiums on the spot, then buy online or by telephone. You can compare quotes for home, motor, travel, boat and caravan insurance.

The Insurance Line　　　　　　　　www.insurance-line.co.uk

A telephone-based company, which deals mainly with motor insurance, but also deals with home insurance. The motor insurance includes motor bikes, classics, fleet, vans, minibus and taxi insurance.

Touchline　　　　　　　　　　　　　www.touchline.co.uk

CHECKLIST

1. Find out your insurance needs – as precisely as possible.

2. Make sure you compare like with like.

3. Explore the Internet for specialist insurance products.

4. Check out brokers to see if they can get you a better deal.

8

Getting Life Assurance on the Internet

UNDERSTANDING LIFE ASSURANCE

Whole life policies

In its simplest and purest form, life assurance is a form of protection. You pay a regular premium to insure your life or someone else's, and when you or they die, your dependants get a lump sum to help them out. However, there has to be an 'insurable interest'. You cannot take out a policy on someone unconnected – say, the President of the United States – and collect a lump sum when he dies.

An 'insurable interest' means that the person has to be someone whose death would cause you financial loss. This is most commonly a family member, but it could be a key person in your business whose death would otherwise cause a financial loss.

This simple form of life assurance is known as a 'whole of life' policy. It can also cover the lives of two people – usually husband and wife – when it is known as a 'joint life' policy.

Term policies

A term policy is one that is taken out only for a certain number of years. If the life assured dies within that period, then the sum assured is paid out. This sort of policy might be taken out to cover mortgage repayments. A level term policy is one where the amount assured stays the same throughout the policy term. A decreasing term policy is one where the sum assured reduces – for example, in line with the reducing amount owing on a mortgage.

Convertible term policies

These are an extension of ordinary term policies. The policy is initially an ordinary term policy, but you have the option at a later date to convert it to an endowment policy. The advantage of this sort of policy is that the 'risk assessment' continues as from the date you originally took out the term policy. If you started a new policy at a later date, you would be that much older, and the premium would be higher.

Critical illness policies

A conventional life assurance pays out when you die. This may be of use to your dependants, but it is, of course, of no use to you. A critical illness policy pays out if you are diagnosed as suffering from one of a range of life-threatening illnesses. Thus, you get some help for the time of this critical illness. This is often a great help to you and your dependants during what can be a distressing time.

Endowment policies

This type of policy is a development of the simple 'protection' type of policy. As well as the protection, there is a savings element, and the policy has a set term. The premiums are, of course, higher, but it guarantees to pay you out. If you die before the end of the policy, it pays out, and if you survive, it also pays out.

With profits policies

Until relatively recently, these were the main type of endowment policies. The money you pay each year is invested by the insurance company, and part of the profits each year are added to the value of your policy – by way of annual bonuses. Once they have been added to the value, they cannot be taken away. When the policy finally matures, a further terminal bonus is added. This bonus is not guaranteed, and tends to fluctuate more than the annual bonuses.

Unitised policies

A more recent development has been unitised policies. The premiums you pay each year are used to buy units in whatever fund you choose, and at the termination of the policy, you get the value of the total number of units credited to you.

USING LIFE ASSURANCE AS SAVINGS

The concept of the endowment policy paved the way for insurance policies to be used in different ways. For instance, mortgage providers developed the endowment mortgage. This meant that you paid the interest only on your mortgage – no capital repayments. At the same time, you paid premiums to a life assurance policy, and at the end of the mortgage term, the proceeds of the policy paid off the mortgage, and usually left you with something extra. The protection element in the life assurance also ensured that if you died, the mortgage was paid off.

Bonds

A bond is a single-premium endowment assurance policy, with a fixed term, or open ended. In return for the single premium you pay at the beginning of the policy, you get either an annual income, plus the return of the premium at the end, or a larger sum at the end of the policy. The tax treatment of these made them more favourable in certain circumstances, and they were heavily marketed by the insurance companies.

WEB SITES

Barclays Life   www.life.barclays.co.uk

This is the life assurance arm of Barclays Bank. The life assurance policies on offer include protection policies and investment bonds for lump sum investment or regular savings. There is a financial check-up section, and '2020 vision'. This is an interesting report by the Henley Centre. It makes some forecasts about what life might be like in the year 2020. Interesting reading, if you are so inclined.

Britannic   www.britannic.co.uk

This is a site with lots of goodies, and it looks smart. The opening screen gives you a new picture of swans each month, and you can download a swans picture to use as wallpaper on your computer. There is a quiz, and competitions with new prizes every month. The company calls its web site 'the home of one-to-one financial advice'.

The life assurance products include protection policies for life and critical illness cover. The bonds and endowment policies cater for lump sum investments or regular savings.

There is a '49ers' section, aimed at those above that age, thinking about or approaching retirement. This is light-hearted, including a '20 things you should know' section, featuring such things as '10 things to do when your kids finally leave home', one of which is 'learn to use the telephone again when your kids finally leave the telephone to you'.

The site also has a personal financial planner, where you can create your personal profile, and enter all the dates of the key events to come in your life.

Clerical Medical   www.clericalmedical.co.uk

This company has a wide range of life assurances and investment bonds. The site is a large one, with many interesting features.

Ecclesiastical Insurance Group   www.eigonline.co.uk

This company was originally formed to deal with the insurance needs of churches and people in churches. It now has a wide variety of products. Its life assurance policies include protection policies for term assurance, convertible term assurance, family income benefit, mortgage protection, permanent health and critical illness insurance. There are various bonds for lump sum investment, and endowment plans for regular savings.

Legal & General   www.landg.com

This is a huge company, and the web site reflects this. The protection policies include policies for whole life, term assurance, illness, income protection and mortgage protection.

The savings section is run by Legal & General Bank, and the investments section features their unit trusts. They market their life assurance bonds through this site.

MGM Assurance   www.mgm-assurance.co.uk

This is a mutual company, and the site is called 'IFA direct'. This means that it is aimed primarily at independent financial advisers. The site features its products generally, but with emphasis on their Retirement Security Account, and their Capital Investment Bond.

Pearl   www.pearl.co.uk

There is no information on this site, merely contact addresses and telephone numbers.

Scottish Amicable   www.scottishamicable.com

This company has an 'AAA' rating from Standard and Poors – the highest rating for financial strength. It naturally trumpets this on its site. The company offers a wide range of products, including investments, life assurance, pensions and ISAs.

This company is the sponsor of the Barbarians rugby club, and the site includes a spot the ball competition, with monthly prizes of rugby shirts.

Scottish Widows   www.scottishwidows.co.uk

This is an attractive and sophisticated site, with many interesting features to look out for. The company has a large range of products and services. The life assurance products include policies for income protection, term assurances, mortgage protection and critical illness cover. The investment type products include endowment plans and the with-profit bond.

Scottish Widows television and newspaper advertising has always featured an attractive woman in a black cape and hood. There have been two of these, Debbie Moore (the daughter of actor Roger Moore) and Amanda Lumb. You can find out more about them on the home page by clicking on 'Which Widow?'

Skandia Life   www.skandia.co.uk

This company offers a wide range of policies, but they will only deal with the public through a professional independent adviser. The site will give you some suggestions if you do not have contact with an independent financial adviser.

Standard Life   www.standardlife.co.uk

This is the largest mutual insurer in Europe. It offers various life assurance products including pure protection policies, mortgage protection and a wide range of investment type bonds. The customer services section of the site enables you to check on current values of your policies or deal with any other queries you may have.

There is also a large section called 'Standard Life – life outlined'. This is a 'lifestyle' section dealing with:

- healthy life   – an exercise planner
  – a height and weight comparative chart
  – women's health
  – eating well – with a recipe of the month
- home life   – gardening calendar
  – toolbox (DIY hints)
  – housebuying tips
  – holidays

- working life
  - a CV writer
  - psychometric test
  - coping with stress
  - interview techniques
- future life
  - achievements of people over 80
  - enjoying retirement
  - life of luxury
  - anniversary reminder
  - pension planner.

All of these have links to other relevant sites. A useful all-round general interest site.

Sun Life	www.axaequityandlaw.co.uk

The Sun Life company is owned by Axa Equity and Law – hence the web site address. The site is updated monthly, and it contains all the information about the company's life assurances, pensions and investments.

Virgin Direct	www.virgin-direct.co.uk

This company claims to have 'taken life assurance back to basics', and offers protection policies. These include a whole of life policy and a mortgage protection policy.

USING BROKERS AND AGENTS

Some brokers and agents specialise in life assurances.

First Global Insurance Services	www.ins-site.co.uk

This site gives a good explanation of life assurance, and deals with the factors to take into account to establish your needs – such things as the ages of you and your partner, the ages of your children, current and potential incomes, living expenses, and so on. Quick quotes are available online, and you can contact them online.

Online Life Assurance Services	www.financial-guidance-centre.co.uk

This is a broker site, aimed mainly at Brits abroad (whom it calls 'Ex-patriots'). It promotes life assurance from UK companies, which are much cheaper than the equivalent cover from a foreign company.

TRADING ENDOWMENT POLICIES

This is a recent development. If you cannot keep up the premiums, or wish to cash in the policy early for any reason, you can surrender the policy to the insurance company, who will pay you a reduced amount.

However, a market has developed for traded endowment policies. This means that instead of surrendering the policy to the company, you sell the policy to another person, who takes over the liability to pay the premiums, then collects the final pay-out. There are several firms active in this market, bringing together those who wish to buy and those who wish to sell.

Association of Policy Market Makers   www.moneyworld.co.uk/apmm

---

This is an association of eight of the biggest companies in this field. The site gives full details of all members.

Absolute Assigned Policies   www.aap.co.uk

This site tells you all you need to know about traded endowment policies – whether you want to cash in a policy, or invest in a second-hand policy.

Insurance Policy Trading Company   www. endowments-direct.co.uk

---

Beale Dobie   www.bealedobie.co.uk

This is one of the leading and longest established companies in this field. It is a subsidiary of Fedsure Investments (UK) Ltd.

The site includes comprehensive sections on selling a policy, and investing in a policy. As well as pointing out the benefits, they make sure that you understand the nature of the investment. They also point out the tax implications of this sort of investment. The site also includes the normal warnings that they only buy and sell policies, and that they cannot advise on the suitability of the product for you, and that the value of the policy depends on future bonus rates, which can go down as well as up.

PolicyPlus   www.policyplus.com

This company, based in Bath, trades in endowment policies. It has a resident cartoon character of a Roman soldier. He is the jargon buster, explaining in plain English the various terms. He will also give you a virtual tour of Bath.

The site has a lengthy explanation of endowment policies, designed to help you understand them, and the 'why all the fuss?' section explains why there has been recent bad publicity about life assurance companies.

Surrenda-link Ltd   www.surrendalink.u-net.com

CHECKLIST

1. Use life assurance for protection for your dependants.

2. You can also use life assurance for savings.

3. You can invest a lump sum or make regular savings.

4. Bonds can carry tax advantages.

5. If you cannot keep up the payments on an endowment policy, you may be able to sell it rather than surrendering it.

6. You can invest in a 'second-hand' endowment policy.

9

Investing on the Internet

UNDERSTANDING INVESTMENTS

For the purpose of this chapter, **saving** means putting your money into an account where you earn interest. That account may give you instant access, or you may have to give a certain amount of notice before you can get your money out. The interest you earn may be at a variable rate, or it may be fixed.

Investing means putting your money into some form of business. It may go directly into the company, if you buy shares, or indirectly, if you invest in a collective investment (such as a unit trust, investment trust, or OEIC). The investment may be in different forms.

Equities

Ordinary shares form what is known as the 'equity' of the company. This means that you are a part owner of the company, sharing in its risks and rewards. The value of the shares can go up or down, with the fortunes of the company. The income on the shares is in the form of dividends, which is really a share in the profit of the company (after retaining some for ploughing back into the business) divided among the owners. The dividend can vary from year to year. Thus, ordinary shares can reward you with a regular income, and growth in the value of the investment – known as capital growth.

Historically, ordinary shares (or 'equities') have provided by far the best investment in the long term. Their capital values have grown far above other forms of investment – including property – and the income from them has tended to show steady growth, combating the effect of inflation.

Preference shares

Preference shares also give you a part ownership of a company. However, the dividend is a fixed rate, and they do not participate in the profits of the company as ordinary shares do. Their fixed rate dividend is a prior charge on the profits of the company, and in the event of a liquidation of the company, they would be paid before any ordinary shares – hence the name 'preference'. These shares do not carry as great a risk as ordinary shares, but neither do they share the same rewards.

Convertibles

These are a special kind of preference share. They pay the fixed rate dividend, but they also confer the right to convert into ordinary shares at a predetermined amount. This right can usually be exercised at a certain time each year for a fixed number of years.

Corporate bonds

This is a form of borrowing by a company. If you have a corporate bond, you are not a shareholder in the company. They usually take the form of a loan with a fixed repayment date, giving a fixed rate of interest. The income you receive is not dividend income, and therefore has a different tax treatment.

BUYING AND SELLING INVESTMENTS

Buying or selling shares as investments is done through a stock exchange. In this book we will talk about the London Stock Exchange. To buy or sell shares, you must deal through a stockbroker. The stockbroker deals on the stock exchange with market makers or through the SETS system.

Market makers are traders who deal only with brokers. The broker approaches a market maker stating that he wants to deal in a particular share. The market maker will quote two prices – one at which he will offer to buy, the other at which he will offer to sell. The difference between the buying and selling price is called the spread, or turn. If a market maker wishes to discourage trading in a certain share, he might quote a large spread. If the broker is satisfied with the price, he tells the market maker the quantity and whether he wants to buy or sell, and the deal is done.

The SETS system is a computerised method of linking offers to buy and offers to sell. Brokers post on the SETS system their offers to buy or sell certain shares, with the prices, and the system matches up buyers and sellers.

Settling the bills

When the deal is done, the broker will issue you with a contract note showing the details of the transaction. Settlement is within five working days. If you have sold, you will have to sign a share transfer, and send this to the broker. He will then send you the proceeds within the five days. If you have bought, you will have to give your personal details to be registered with the company, and you must pay the broker within the five working days.

If you want to find out more about the London Stock Exchange from the horse's mouth, go to their web site

The London Stock Exchange	www.londonstockex.co.uk

This is a useful site, with many useful links to other sites which you may find helpful.

DAY TRADING

This is a form of trading which has recently come to the forefront of news and comment. It consists of trading stocks and shares on the same day, in the hope of large price movements on that day, to try to turn a profit. In practice, the best intelligence suggests that about 70 per cent of those carrying out day trading actually lose money on it, and only a tiny proportion of those making a profit make anything worth writing home about.

This form of trading started in America, but it is taking hold in the UK. One of the main reasons people are able to day trade is the existence of detailed and instant information on the Internet.

Day Trading Stocks.com	www.daytradingstocks.com

This is an American web site devoted to day trading. It includes information to learn the elements of day trading, help to get you started, and a chat room, to talk to other day traders.

CHOOSING AND USING A BROKER

You can find a stockbroker on the web. However, probably the best way to find one is through a personal recommendation. If you have a friend or relation who uses a stockbroker, ask their candid opinion of their service. Alternatively, an accountant or solicitor will probably be able to recommend one. Once you have a stockbroker, stay with them unless there is some serious problem. The relationship you build up over the years will prove very useful.

The service you get from your broker can be:

- advisory
- execution only
- discretionary.

Advisory

This means that the broker advises you when you request advice on, say, whether to sell, or investing a lump sum. He might also contact you when he feels that buying or selling a particular share might be a good move.

Execution only

This means that the broker will make a certain transaction for you, simply on your instructions. He may have no opinion, or he may advise against it, but if you give the order to go ahead, he will carry out your request.

Discretionary

This means that you give the broker the right to manage your shares. The broker will hold your shares in a nominee company, in an account designated in your name. He will then make any deals which he considers right for you. In order to do this, he will start by finding out your requirements – for example, whether you are interested mainly in income, or capital growth, or a mixture of both. He will also have other information – about your age, other circumstances, etc. that will be relevant to the management of your shares.

LOW COST AND INTERNET DEALING

There are many companies offering low cost and internet dealing. They will carry out sales or purchases of shares on the Stock Exchange for a low commission or a fixed fee. (Brokers usually charge a commission – a percentage of the amount of the deal.) These low-cost dealers include banks and stockbrokers operating on an execution-only basis.

The sites often include:

- news about companies which may be useful to investors
- price histories of individual shares

- detailed analysis of share prices and the indexes
- graphs and charts
- online demonstration
- real time quotes before you trade.

You will be asked to register as a customer before you can trade, in much the same way as if you were using a stockbroker. Some sites offer other premium services for extra information, which are subject to a small monthly payment.

Barclays Stockbrokers   www.barclays-stockbrokers.co.uk

This is the stockbroking arm of Barclays Bank. This site also offers advisory dealing, and a section on investment clubs.

Charles Schwab Europe   www.schwab-worldwide.com

This site is part of the Charles Schwab Corporation group. It offers dealing in the US market as well as the UK market, and also offers the first 30 days' trading free of commission.

CMC   www.forex-cmc.com

This site offers futures and options trading online as well as share trading. It also has a live chat line.

DLJ Direct   www.dljdirect.co.uk

This site is owned by Donaldson, Lufkin and Jenrette, an American firm of brokers (who describe themselves as a 'Wall Street power-house'). They offer US and UK dealing, with an initial free of commission offer. You can also create a 'model portfolio' without committing any funds, to try your hand at investing and see how your choices perform against the index.

E Cortal   www.e-cortal.co.uk

E*TRADE UK LTD   www.etrade.co.uk

This site has many features. There is RE*SEARCH, which provides share price information and free quotes, and other portfolio tools, from £5 plus VAT per month. One section of the site gives late breaking news about companies. There is a 'community' section to share news and views with other investors, and access to other E*TRADE sites around the world.

FasTrade   www.fastrade.co.uk

This company works on a commission of 0.5 per cent, with a minimum £15 charge. It requires shares to be held in their FasTrade Stock Account before they can be sold, and cleared funds to be held in your FasTrade deposit account before they can buy.

Halifax   www.halifax.co.uk/sharedeal

This service is called the ShareXpress online. You must register, and you are then given a PIN. This enables you to deal over the Internet, with the advantages of:

- complete online dealing
- immediate price confirmation
- free stock market information
- competitive commission rates
- no management or administration charges
- view your portfolio online
- 128-bit encryption for security
- shares held electronically in the Halifax nominee name.

You can also buy or sell an ISA on this service.

James Brearley & Sons Ltd   www.brearley.iii.co.uk

myBROKER   www.mybroker.co.uk

NatWest Stockbrokers   www.natweststockbrokers.co.uk

You must register to deal online, but non-members can still access the information service. The dealing service is an execution only service, available 24 hours a day, for UK stocks only. Share prices are displayed with a 15-minute delay, and there is a full information service on all UK listed companies.

RT2 Trader   www.rt2trader.co.uk

This site originates from the USA, and it is one which is used by people for day trading.

Stocktrade   www.stocktrade.co.uk

This is the Internet site of Brewin Dolphin, a member of the London Stock Exchange. It includes a section of links to other useful financial sites.

Xest   www.xest.com

This is the Internet site of Charles Stanley & Co. Ltd, a member of the London Stock Exchange. It includes a useful 'financial links' section, and a bookshop section.

TAKING AN ACTIVE INTEREST

You may also want to take more of an active interest in your shares, and in the market generally. You can do this to manage your shares yourself. You can also, of course, still take an active interest if your shares are managed by a broker.

Understanding the index

In order to get an overall view of the way share prices are moving, and trends, indexes are published. The most commonly used are the ones published by the *Financial Times*. They publish many indexes, of which probably the most commonly used and well known is the FTSE 100 index. This is an index of the prices of the 100 biggest companies traded on the London Stock Exchange. Here are some of the other indexes published by the *Financial Times*:

- FT 30 Index – the top 30 companies
- FTSE 250 Index – the top 250 companies
- FTSE 350 Index – the top 350 companies
- FTSE All Share Index – all the shares traded on the London Stock Exchange
- FTSE Non Financials Index – all the shares except financial

(banks, insurance companies etc.); these excluded shares often have a different price pattern from other shares, and seeing the index of shares apart from these can give particular insights
* FTSE Fixed Interest Index – fixed interest stocks
* FTSE Government Securities Index – government securities.

The movement of these indexes can be shown on a graph over any period of time, and provide a useful analysis tool – for example, to compare the price movement of one particular share to a relevant index. The index is also used to show a correlation between share prices and other factors – say, the movement of interest rates.

Collective investment management companies also use these indexes. A common line used in marketing is 'how many unit/ investment trusts have out-performed the FTSE 100?'

Reading the prices
Prices are shown daily in most newspapers, and you can also get share prices on the Internet – with various degrees of delay from 'real time'. The most complete list of prices is in the *Financial Times*. Prices will be shown for each share individually. The shares are classified according to their sector, and include such sectors of the economy as: Alcoholic beverages, Banks, Breweries, Building materials, Chemicals – listed alphabetically through to Telecommunications, Transport and Water.

The information given will usually include:

* *Price*   This is the mid-price at the end of the previous day.
* *+ or –*   This is the movement of the price from the previous day.
* *52 week high/low*   This is the highest and lowest prices in the previous 52 weeks.
* *Market capitalisation*   This is the total number of ordinary shares in issue multiplied by the price.
* *Yield %*   This is the real return you would get on the share if you bought at the price given.
* *P/E*   This is the price/earnings ratio – a key indicator.

Spotting a good thing
Once you know your way round the stock market, you will be able to develop a 'nose' for a good investment. There are various factors to

take into account.

Market sector
You must take a view, and take advice, on what sector of the market will perform well. Will it be telecommunications, or information technology, banking or insurance, leisure or media? This involves knowing not only about the market, but also about the world and business generally, then trying to spot where future gains will come from.

Price/earnings ratio
This key indicator shows the price of a share in relationship to the earnings per share (i.e. the profit of the company divided between the number of shares in the company).

> *Example:*
> A company has profits of £3 million. It has 10 million shares in issue. Its earnings per share are 30p. If the price quoted for that share is £3, then the price/earnings ratio is ten. That means the price of the share represents ten years' profits. Note that this does not necessarily mean ten years' dividends. Usually, the company will have to keep back some of its profits to plough back into the business.

Quality of earnings
The price/earnings ratio is, of course, based on historic figures. This information is obviously not as important to the investor as future profits. As we do not know the future, we have to depend on the analysts. These are people employed by brokers to investigate companies, and their future prospects. Their collective views on companies are known as 'market sentiment'.

If market sentiment about a company is doubtful, the quality of earnings is said to be poor.

Earnings growth
This is a measure of how a company's performance has improved – or otherwise. If the earnings per share have shown steady growth, the company has obviously improved its performance year on year. If there is a dip for one year in an otherwise steady increase, there may well be a good reason. If the earnings per share show a steady decline, ask searching questions before investing your money in it.

Using analysis tools

Various web sites have tools for analysing the price movements, which may or may not help you make a decision. These sort of tools are for those who want to take their destiny into their own hands, and make their own investment decisions.

Updata   www.updata.co.uk

This company supplies investment software and up-to-date information. Worth a visit. (See Figure 15)

Stockwiz   www.stockwiz.com

This is an American site, which 'turns computing power into investing power'. It does this by statistical analysis of the prices of thousands of publicly traded companies. Being an American site, it deals with American companies.

OTHER MARKETS

The London Stock Exchange is the principal market in this country for dealing in shares. In order for a company to qualify for its shares to be traded on the London Stock Exchange, it has to meet stringent requirements. Just below the level of the London Stock Exchange are the Alternative Investment Market, and the Unlisted Securities Market (AIM and USM respectively).

Companies which are quoted on these markets are not quite as marketable as ones on the London Stock Exchange, but they are often the stepping stone to 'full marketability'.

NASDAQ   www.nasdaq.com

This is an American exchange which has opened trading exchanges in other parts of the world. After setting up in Hong Kong, it made a beeline for London. This exchange is widely recognised and used for trading in information technology-based shares.

CHOOSING A COLLECTIVE INVESTMENT

Many companies use their web site as an advertising hoarding. Amongst these are investment companies. As long as you realise that the web site is only an extension of the sort of advertisements they would put in a newspaper, you need not be overawed by the complexity of some of the sites.

As required by the regulatory body, the sites must include the warnings about values of investments being liable to fall as well as increase. Make sure you understand the nature of the regulatory statements on each site.

Most companies offering investments in such things as unit trusts or investment trusts will give up-to-date prices of their funds, and historical information about each fund's performance. Most also give more detailed information about the management of each fund, and what investments are included under the umbrella.

There is also no shortage of information about ISAs, and PEP transfers, and most sites will have a page on 'how to invest' and one on frequently asked questions.

UNIT TRUST AND INVESTMENT TRUST COMPANIES

Aberdeen Asset Management	www.aberdeen-asset.co.uk

This investment group has a wide range of unit trusts and investment trusts, including UK-based funds, US-based funds, European, Far East, and specialist funds.

The specialist funds include an Ethical Fund and a High Yield Bond ISA.

The site has an 'ISAs explained' section, and prices on all the trusts at 12 noon are posted the next working day on the site. There is also a weekly market briefing, with sections on markets in the UK, USA, Europe, other parts of the world, and a global report.

Dresdner RCM Global Investors	www.dresdnerrcm.co.uk

Exeter Fund Managers	www.chameleon-isa.co.uk

This company is a smaller but good quality manager of funds. It manages several ranges of funds, including one for zero preference shares.

Its chameleon portfolios put together different selections of unit trust funds to create specialist portfolios. For instance, there is a monthly income portfolio, combining three Exeter funds to give a good annualised rate of return, with monthly interest.

Fidelity	www.fidelity.co.uk

This is a large group, with over 15 million investors. It offers unit trusts and investment trusts. The site gives information on all its investments which include ISAs, unit trusts and investment trusts. You can also invest online, and the site has interactive tools.

Fleming Asset Management	www.flemings.co.uk

Foreign and Colonial	www.fandc.co.uk

This is the world's largest international investment trust. They were the first ever investment trust, having launched the first fund in 1868.

Framlington	www.framlington.co.uk

This is an investment trust.

Friends Provident	www.friendsprovident.co.uk

This investment company was started by Quakers (the Religious Society of Friends) and maintains its strong ethical stance. It has several funds, and one of the main features is the 'stewardship' range of ethical investments. This range of investments can be tailored to:

- lump sum investment
- paying off your mortgage
- retirement planning.

There is also an 'ethical investment' newsletter.

Gartmore	www.gartmore.iii.co.uk

This company is the investment arm of the NatWest Group. The home page is designed a little differently from most. The prompts are:

- to look at investments
- to read about Gartmore
- the Gartmore service for professional advisers

- to request literature or contact them.

The company has unit trusts, investment trusts, ISAs and pensions on its product list.

Henderson   www.henderson.com

This company has unit trusts and investment trusts as its products, with ISA options. Under each heading, there is a helpful page called 'your decision'. This helps you find the right trust, by prompting you to choose information on:

- income
- capital growth
- income and growth
- specialist trusts.

You can get further fact sheets or brochures from the site, check the performance and prices of the funds, and buy online.

Jupiter   www.jupiteronline.co.uk

This company has a well-performing range of trusts. The first screen gives all the regulations and warning statements, which you must go through before you can get into the home page. The web site shows the range of funds, with detailed information on each, and regularly updated prices of each fund. The information is quite detailed. If you are thinking of investing in one of their funds, this is a good place to start. There is also the information you would expect about ISAs and transferring PEP funds.

M and G   www.mandg.co.uk

This large unit trust company has details about its many funds, information about ISAs and transferring PEPs. Prices are updated every day, and there is information on how to buy and sell.

Martin Currie   www.martincurrie.com

This is one of Scotland's oldest and largest independent investment management groups.

Their products include:

- unit trusts
- OEICs
- investment trusts
- offshore funds

There are services for:

- individual investors
- advisers
- institutional investors.

The investment funds cover UK, International, North America, Japan, Far East, Europe, Emerging Markets and Specialist Funds.

Mercury Asset Management   www.mam.com

Perpetual   www.perpetual.co.uk

This is a large and successful investment group. Its products include unit trusts, investment trusts, ISAs and pensions. The company, quite naturally, trumpets its own successes, with details of recent major awards. You can get up-to-date fund prices and market reports. If you want to find out who is in charge of your money, there are profiles of the various fund managers. You can also download any of the literature you need from the site.

Schroder   www.schroder.co.uk

The web site is simple, and perhaps a bit on the dull side. However, it sets out simply the details of the company's funds. For serious investors, there are:

- weekly news of global markets
- monthly investment review
- quarterly review of funds
- fund prices updated daily
- strategic management service.

There is also the usual information about ISAs and transferring PEPs.

Threadneedle Investments	www.threadneedle.co.uk

This is another large unit trust company. Their web site includes all the information about their funds, a news summary of stockmarkets, and a monthly strategy guide. You can visit their 'ISA centre'. It also includes a very brief explanation of the ratings given by Standard and Poor's – both the Micropal and the Fund Research.

INSURANCE COMPANIES

Many insurance companies offer collective investments.

Clerical Medical	www.clericalmedical.co.uk

This company has a range of unit trusts. The site has a useful feature which advises you on the sort of investments which may suit you for different stages of life, including:

- further education
- life in retirement
- planning a family.

The company also publishes a guide to retirement, which you can request by phone on 0800 779077 or by email on the web site.

Legal & General	www.landg.com

This site has a section devoted to helping you understand investments, and information on their full range of unit trusts.

CHECKLIST

1. Understand what the different types of investment are.

2. Don't put all your eggs in one basket.

3. Find out all you can about the way to buy and sell investments.

4. Find a broker or adviser.

5. You can deal on the Internet.

6. Take an active interest in your investments.

7. Think about collective investments.

10

Using Tax Incentives in Investment

ISAs

The main tax incentive at present is the Individual Savings Account. Any income and capital growth on these accounts is free of any tax in this country. In the first tax year of their introduction, the 1999/2000 tax year, you could invest a maximum of £7,000 in an ISA. The same limit applies for 2000/2001, but thereafter the maximum annual investment will be £5,000.

An ISA investment can be in one or all of three types of investment (called ISA elements):

- *Cash* – an account with a bank, building society, insurance company or National Savings.

- *Stocks and shares* – which can include shares, unit trusts, investment trusts, OEICs, government stocks and corporate bonds.

- *Insurance* – certain types of life assurance policies.

You may invest in Maxi ISAs or Mini ISAs.

- A *Maxi ISA* can be up to the full amount of the annual investment, and can be invested in stocks and shares alone, or stocks and shares plus one or both of the other ISA elements.

- You may invest in up to three *Mini ISA*s in each tax year. A Mini ISA can only be invested in one of the three elements, and is subject to the folloing limits in each tax year:

– *cash*	maximum of £3,000 in the 1999/2000 and 2000/2001 tax years, £1,000 thereafter
– *stocks and shares*	maximum of £3,000
– *insurance*	maximum of £1,000
– *overall limit*	maximum of £7,000 in the 1999/2000 and 2000/2001 tax years, £5,000 thereafter.

CAT standards

This is a government-approved measure of Charges, Access and Terms. If the providers of ISAs meet the standards, they are allowed to promote their products as CAT standard. The CAT standard does not imply any other approval of the product, nor does it give any sort of guarantee. Indeed, there may be many investments which do not meet the CAT standards, but which still offer good value, and suitability for your needs.

Providers

There are many ISA providers, mainly banks, building societies, insurance companies, unit trusts, investment trusts and OEICs. The following is a list of some of the ISA providers. For most of them, fuller details of their web site are in Chapter 9, so no further information is given here.

Aberdeen Unit Trusts   www.aberdeen-asset.com

A wide range of ISAs is available, mirroring their range of unit trusts and investment trusts.

Fidelity   www.webxpress.fidelity.co.uk

The ISA from Fidelity is called ISAXpress, and the web site address is different from the main address of Fidelity. You can invest online.

Gartmore   www.gartmore.iii.co.uk

The site answers frequently asked questions about ISAs, and gives a wide choice of ISAs:

- Global ISA – a choice of 15 unit trusts
- UK Index ISA – an index tracking fund
- ISAit – a choice of 14 investment trust ISAs.

Henderson Investors   www.henderson.com

There is an ISA guide, with questions and answers, and a link to Henderson's 'Selection ISA'. The site is liberally scattered with 'uplifting thoughts'.

Hill Samuel   www.isa2000.co.uk

This is a web site dedicated to this one product – the ISA 2000.

Invesco   www.gtglobal.co.uk

This company offers ISAs in unit trusts and investment trusts, and enables you to invest in almost any region of the world.

Jupiter   www.jupiteronline.co.uk

The full range of funds are available as ISAs, with investment in funds slanted towards income, growth, fixed interest or international funds.

Legal & General   www.landg.com

This giant company has a range of unit trusts among its products. There are equity-based unit trusts and fixed interest ones on offer as ISAs, and you can also invest a TESSA maturity ISA with them.

Newton Fund Managers   www.newton.co.uk

Perpetual Investment Management Services   www.perpetual.co.uk

The funds previously available as PEPs are now available as ISAs, plus a further two funds, due to the fact that ISAs now carry no geographical restrictions.

Royal and SunAlliance   www.rsa-investments.co.uk

RSA offers 13 actively managed funds, a European fund, a FTSE 100 Tracker fund (this one meets the CAT standard) and a North American fund.

Schroders   www.schroder.co.uk

The site gives you all the information you need about ISAs, with application forms. Their ISA product is called the Schroder MaximISA.

Threadneedle Investments   www.threadneedle.co.uk

Threadneedle have a choice of 25 investment funds for ISAs, and four risk-rated managed funds. Their '3-IN-1 Income Solution' is an ISA split into three funds:

- High Yield Bond Fund – 50 per cent
- Monthly Extra Income Fund – 25 per cent
- UK Monthly Income Fund – 25 per cent.

This offers a competitive level of tax free income, with a potential for capital growth.

FRIENDLY SOCIETIES

Friendly Societies are able to issue 'tax exempt life or endowment policies'. These are a form of life assurance used mainly for savings purposes. There is a maximum limit of £25 per month, or £270 yearly, on the premiums payable. However, within this modest limit, all gains on these policies are free of tax.

Exeter Friendly Society   www.exeterfriendly.co.uk

This society majors on offering health insurance.

Family Assurance   www.family.co.uk

This claims to be the biggest tax-exempt Friendly Society in the UK. They have over 500,000 members.

There is a bulletin board, with company news and community news. There are regular competitions on the board, and you can enter an 'ethical share race' by making a 'virtual portfolio' and checking its progress against others in the race. The leader board is shown on the bulletin board.

The site has detailed information about its products, and the various funds.

Friend Indeed Friendly Society   www.friend-indeed.co.uk

This is a new Friendly Society offering a unique form of insurance cover. Their sole aim is to provide comfort and care for victims of violent crime.

Holloway Friendly Society	www.holloway.co.uk

This society features permanent health insurance, and 10-year savings plans. The site is aimed at independent financial advisers, but you can pick up useful information from it.

Homeowners Friendly Society	www.homeowners.co.uk

This has adults' savings plans, children's savings plans and life assurances. It also features a history of Friendly Societies.

Liverpool Victoria	www.lvbestbonds.co.uk

This also claims to be the biggest Friendly Society, with over 1 million members. The company offers a 'Mutual Investment Bond', tax-free savings, pensions, motor and home insurance, personal loans and a credit card. The credit card and personal loans are provided by arrangement with Frizzell Bank Ltd, and the motor and home insurance are provided by Frizzell Financial Services Ltd.

Royal Liver Assurance	www.royal-liver.com

This society has over 1 million members, and offers savings and investments, personal insurances, pensions, life assurance, mortgage linked insurances, motor and home insurance. There is a competition, and a couple of general interest sections: 'millennium madness' and 'strange lives'.

Scottish Friendly Society	www.scottishfriendly.co.uk

This society offers tax free investments, lump sum investments, life assurance and ISAs.

Tunstall Assurance Society	www.tunstallassurance.co.uk

This Friendly Society is situated in Stoke on Trent. Its savings plan is called the Potters Pride. Its other main claim to fame is that it sponsors Port Vale Football Club.

PENSIONS

We saw in Chapter 6 how important it is to start saving for a pension.

The government acknowledges this, and gives tax concessions on investments in pension funds. If you are employed or self-employed, you get tax relief at your top rate of tax for contributions you make to pension schemes.

When you take the benefits from your pension scheme, you may take a certain proportion of the fund as a tax-free lump sum.

The government is widening the scope of pension provisions eligible for tax breaks by introducing the stakeholder pensions.

NATIONAL SAVINGS

We have already seen in Chapter 3 the National Savings web site. National Savings have many different products. Some of them give tax-free income or interest. These include:

- Premium Bonds – all prizes are free of any tax
- Savings Certificates – the interest and bonuses added at the maturity are free of tax
- Ordinary Account Interest – the first £70 each year of interest on National Savings Bank Ordinary Accounts is free of tax.

CHECKLIST

To get the advantage of government-sponsored tax breaks, invest in:

1. ISAs

2. Friendly Societies

3. pensions

4. some National Savings products.

11

Looking at Alternative Investments

There are a number of investment opportunities which are not 'conventional'. Many people fight shy of these, simply because they do not understand them. Here is a basic principle of investment:

Do not invest in something you do not understand.

Here are a few unconventional investment ideas, with brief explanations.

HOME INCOME PLANS

Many people have a lot of money tied up in their house, which they cannot use in any way. They are said to be 'asset rich, but cash poor'. There is a way in which the value tied up in a house can be released to provide extra income. These plans are issued by investment and insurance companies. They take a part ownership of your house, or a mortgage secured on your house, and the money released can then be used to generate an income. The plans are available to people over 65 years of age. The final day of reckoning does not occur until you die.

Obviously, if you are considering this, you will want a high degree of security, to know that you cannot be thrown out of your house. One of the most basic forms of security is in the amount you can realise. This amount is geared to your age, or the combined ages of husband and wife. The proportion of the value of your house which can be released is very low, probably not more than 30 per cent.

The other main security feature is the wording of the contract which you sign. Make sure that you examine it carefully and, if necessary, give it to a solicitor to examine. Make sure, also, that the company you deal with subscribes to the SHIP (Safe Home Income Plans) code of practice.

Here are some questions to ask about any plan you are considering:

- Are any survey, valuation fees etc. reimbursed by the company?
- Is the scheme transferable if you move house?
- Repairs and insurance – who is responsible?
- Will it affect any Social Security benefits you receive?
- What do your family think about it?
- What would happen if you took out the plan as an unmarried person, then married?
- What would happen if you took out the plan as a married couple, and one of you died?
- What would happen if a family member or friend moved in to care for you or provide companionship?
- What is the minimum age?
- What is the maximum loan to valuation?
- What is the minimum property value?
- Is there any restriction on the type of property, e.g. house, flat, maisonette?

Here are some companies providing home income plans:

Allchurches Life Assurance Ltd	www.eigonline.co.uk

This is part of the Ecclesiastical Insurance Group, which is owned by a charitable trust.

BPT Bridgewater (Home Reversions) Ltd	www.bpt-bridgewater.co.uk

This company belongs to the Bradford Property Trust.

Carlyle Life	www.jhb.co.uk

This company pioneered one of the earliest schemes in 1965. It is a subsidiary of the Julian Hodge Bank.

Home and Capital Trust	www.homecapital.co.uk

This is a reversion company. The plan works by an investor buying the house (at less than the market value) and leasing it back to you rent free for the rest of your life. There can also be a partial reversion – whereby the investor buys a proportion of the house. That means that there is still some value left to your survivors when you die.

You can get an online quotation, and your security is guaranteed by the company. The questions and answers cover most of the queries. This company subscribes to the SHIP code of practice.

Investment Property Reversions Ltd   www.investprop-reversions.com

---

This site is aimed at people who want to invest in a reversion property. The company is a member of the National Association of Estate Agents. This site emphasises the investment opportunities of reversion properties. It answers many of the problems of security, from the point of view of the investor.

NPI In-Retirement Services   Tel: 01892 515151

This company does not have a web site. The NPI (National Provident Institution) is a large insurance and pension company, with assets over 11 billion, and over 600,000 members.

Safe Home Income Plans Ltd   www.ship-ltd.co.uk

This is the site of Safe Homes Income Plans Ltd. The site tells you all about safe plans, and what you should think about before taking out a plan. There are also links to the member companies which have web sites.

Stalwart Assurance Co. Ltd   www.ifap.co.uk/stalwart_assurance.htm

---

This company is owned by the General Electric Company of the USA. It has been offering home income plans since 1986.

DERIVATIVES

These are also known as options, but the term 'derivatives' can also embrace other things such as futures, contracts for differences, swaps, etc. The essence of derivatives is that you have the opportunity to benefit (or lose) from an underlying 'position' (such as the movement in the price of a share) without complete exposure to the position. In plain language, that means you can benefit from the increase in the price of shares (or lose from the reduction in their price) without actually owning them.

The simplest form of this is the 'option'. An 'option' is an agreement by which you pay a price (known as the option premium) for the right to buy or sell shares at a fixed price within a certain time-scale. These agreements also limit the number of shares to be traded under the agreement. If you do not exercise your option within the time-scale, you have lost the rights under that agreement. If you exercise your rights, the person to whom you paid the premium must fulfil their side of the bargain to buy from you or sell to you.

The types of option are:

- *calls* – this gives you the right to buy shares
- *puts* – this gives you the right to sell the shares
- *doubles* – this gives you the right either to buy or sell, but not both.

This form of trading is recognised on the London Stock Exchange, and shares in any company quoted on the London Stock Exchange may be the subject of a traditional options contract. Many brokers will offer this service.

Options Direct (Europe) Ltd   www.options-direct.co.uk

This is a specialist brokerage service, and they have recently started dealing in futures as well as traditional options. They are keen to welcome the seasoned trader and the beginner. The client services they offer include:

- daily market report
- daily trading recommendations updated each morning
- daily positions and portfolio valuations
- live position system so their traders will always know your position.

COLLECTIBLES

Most people have in childhood collected things – stamps, football programmes, teddy bears, dolls – in fact, almost anything. Many collectors take these things into adult life, and other sorts of collections are only developed in adult life. These can include such things as fine wines, antiquarian books, paintings, and so on.

Most collections come about through an interest in the items. They are an interest first, and an investment only secondly. Some collections may be built up by spending time at car boot sales and the like; others may need serious buying at auctions or specialist shops.

Collectibles do, of course, have a physical existence. That means that they need to be kept somewhere. Some items may need special storage conditions, such as a cool wine cellar. Some items, such as pictures, may need to be displayed and lit to be properly appreciated. Some may even be of such importance that they are loaned to a local or national museum for display. Some items will have a special value, and need to be protected. This may mean special anti-burglary precautions. If you are a serious collector, your normal household insurance will probably not cover your collection for loss or damage, and you may have to pay extra for insurance.

Collections suffer from one obvious disadvantage – they do not produce an income. Therefore, in order to benefit from them in a financial sense, you will have to realise their value in some way. This may mean having to part with something to which you have become attached.

On the Internet, look out for the auctioneers' sites. You may be wary about spending money over the Internet on items which you have not seen. Reputable auctioneers have a guarantee of authenticity and condition. They may also have an insurance scheme to cover claims from buyers or sellers.

Bonhams	www.bonhams.com
Christie's	www.christies.com
Gavelnet. com	www.gavelnet.com
Phillips	www.phillips-auctions.com
Sotheby's	www.sothebys.com
Sotheby's have also recently joined up with amazon at	www.sothebys.amazon.com
Tennants	www.tennants.co.uk

Other dealers and fairs have web sites, such as:

Olympia Fine Art and Antiques Fair	www.olympia-antiques.co.uk
Glade Antiques	www.gladeantiques.com
Contemporary Art Society	www.contempart.org.uk
ART2000	www.art-fair.co.uk
Will's Art Warehouse	www.wills-art.com

Online auctions can be accessed for almost anything you want to buy. Here are some of the auction sites:

Qxl	www.qxl.com
Ebay	www.ebay.com/uk
Ebid	www.ebid.co.uk
Yahoo	www.auctions.yahoo.com/uk

ETHICAL INVESTMENTS

More and more people these days are thinking about ethical investments. Some investments promote positive ethical or 'green' agendas, such as:

- energy and resource conservation
- recycling
- renewable energy
- pollution control
- free-range foods
- sustainable agriculture and forestry
- minimising waste
- environmental technology
- public transport
- fair trade with Third World countries.

Other investments have a negative side, avoiding such things as:

- tobacco
- alcohol
- arms trade
- exploitation of Third World countries
- heavy pollution
- animal testing
- pornography
- environmental damage.

Many of the 'greenest' and most ethical companies perform well, and you do not necessarily have to accept a lower return on your investment for the sake of your conscience. **However, ethical**

investments are not necessarily low risk.

Here is a list of some companies which have ethical investments – we have already seen their web sites in other chapters:

Co-operative Bank	www.co-operativebank.co.uk
Friends Provident	www.friendsprovident.co.uk
Jupiter	www.jupiteronline.co.uk
Triodos Bank	www.triodos.co.uk

CHECKLIST

1. You can raise money from the value of your house.

2. Derivatives and options are an alternative, higher-risk form of investing.

3. Collectibles can provide an interest as well as financial gain.

4. Invest ethically – but it is not necessarily low risk.

12

Paying your Taxes on the Internet

The government is promoting ways for us to deal with, and pay, our taxes on the Internet. You can already access the Inland Revenue and the Customs and Excise.

INLAND REVENUE AND THE CUSTOMS AND EXCISE

Inland Revenue www.inlandrevenue.gov.uk

The site is friendly and helpful – perhaps not the first thing you would associate with the Inland Revenue! However, that cuddly cartoon character, Hector the Inspector, is there to guide you round the site. It has sections about:

- self assessment, both for income tax and corporation tax
- the Construction Industry scheme
- National Insurance contributions
- electronic business
- employer's pack online
- Gift Aid 2000
- tax credits for working families and disabled persons.

The site is truly user friendly, and very helpful. For instance, in the section about Self Assessment, there is advice on how to complete the tax return. You may download the electronic version, to fill in your return on your computer – and from April 2000 you are able to submit it over the Internet. You can see what happens once you send in your tax return. There is advice about what records you must keep, how long to keep them, and how to get hold of records if they are lost.

You can print out and keep a chart to see the deadlines to remember. You can see the twelve most common mistakes (and how to avoid them), and general tips on Self Assessment. There is also a list of tax offices and enquiry centres, and you can read the Taxpayers' Charter.

You can download forms, leaflets and booklets, tax bulletins, and a summary of tax rates and allowances. There is also a set of links to other useful sites.

Customs and Excise	www.hmce.gov.uk

If you are in business, the chances are that you are registered for VAT. This site deals with other Customs and Excise duties as well, but the main point of interest is VAT. You can seek advice from Customs and Excise about VAT, and there is a link to the newly designed online VAT return which you can use to make your returns via the Internet.

USING ADVISERS

You can access private tax return services online, and tax advisers, many of whom are Chartered or Certified Accountants. There are a large number, ready and waiting to advise you. The Financial Intermediaries Network Directory has several pages listing accountants and tax advisers – nearly 300 of them – at www.find.co.uk/advice/AAC.html.

If you want to be sure that an adviser is properly regulated and qualified, you can check the web sites of the major regulators.

Association of Chartered Certified Accountants	www.acca.co.uk

Besides information about the Association, you can click on 'Find an Accountant'.

The Chartered Institute of Taxation	http://193.130.13.244

There is much information on this site, divided neatly between these categories:

- information for the taxpaying public
- information for professional advisers
- information for students of tax.

Click on an area of the country to obtain a list of accountants in that area.
Or click on an area from the list below.
To Search the site by keywords click here.

KEY

* This symbol by an entry indicates that the firm is not composed wholly of members belonging to the three
Institutes of Chartered Accountants in Great Britain and Ireland.

DISTRICTS

London Central.	London North.	London East.	London S.E.
London South.	London S.W.	London N.W.	Canterbury.
Maidstone.	Tunbridge Wells.	Brighton.	Portsmouth.
Isle of Wight.	Southampton.	Bournemouth.	Taunton.
Devon.	Cornwall.	Bristol.	Reading.
Guildford.	Gatwick.	Southend.	Colchester.
Norwich.	Cambridge.	Harlow.	Watford.
Bedford.	Oxford.	Gloucester.	Cardiff.
Swansea.	Shrewsbury.	West Midlands.	Wolverhampton.
Birmingham North.	Birmingham South.	Birmingham Central.	Coventry.
Northampton.	Peterborough.	Leicester.	Nottingham.
Derby.	Chesterfield.	Stoke.	North Wales.
Chester & Wirral.	Merseyside.	Manchester South.	Manchester Central.
Manchester North	Bolton.	Sheffield.	Lincoln.
York.	Huddersfield.	Leeds.	Bradford.
Blackburn.	Preston.	Cumbria.	Middlesbrough.
Sunderland.	Newcastle.	Edinburgh.	Scotland S.W.
Glasgow South.	Glasgow North.	Dundee.	Aberdeen.
Highlands.	Northern Ireland.	Isle of Man	Channel Islands
Other Areas.			

Fig. 12. Chartered Accountants directory map.

Chartered Accountants	www.chartered-accountants.co.uk

This site has links to the individual sites of the institutes in England and Wales, Ireland, and Scotland. This combined site will direct you to a Chartered Accountant, either by searching the directory of firms alphabetically, or by clicking on a geographical location (see Figure 12). With so many advisers to choose from, we cannot list all of them in this book. Here is a small sample.

Accountax Consulting	www.accountax-ltd.co

This is a specialist tax consultancy. It specialises in fighting status cases. These occur when employers (particularly in the construction industry) are told to reclassify their subcontractors as employed people. This means the Inland Revenue and the Social Security Contributions Agency can collect a lot more money.

Accountax specialises in fighting these cases, and their boast is that they have never lost a case yet. They offer individual consultancy, seminars and a 'fighting fund'. This is really a subscription to their services on an annual basis, giving various benefits, including discounts. This service is likely to be of most value to accountants.

Etax Ltd	www.etax.co.uk

This company offers a same-day tax return completion service. You send your details (password protected) and they will prepare the return and send it to the Inland Revenue electronically. There is an email helpline, and the costs start at £65.

Murray Noble Ltd	www.rebatecheck.co.uk

This web site is aimed at those who think they are paying too much tax – and don't we all think that? The site prompts you to check online whether you are due for a rebate, by entering in your personal details, income, etc. There are examples of tax claims you could make, and a couple of pages of long-term tax-saving strategies.

13

Reading All About It

If you are serious about handling your finances, whether on the Internet or not, you will no doubt want to keep in touch as much as you can with the latest news, innovations and advice. There are many journals and magazines to help you, and many of them are online – in fact, some of them only exist online.

Many of the best known names in the world of financial journals and magazines are present on the Internet. Some of them require registration, but generally this is free of charge. They are all liberally scattered with advertising hoardings, which say in a thousand seductive ways 'come on – click on me!' Practically all of them have bookshops which offer you discounted books on financial subjects.

Perhaps the most famous financial paper in the world is the *Financial Times*.

Financial Times	www.ft.com

This does not require registration, and allows you access to all the news and comment (general and financial) which you will find in the paper version, as well as a large research and data section, including:

- global archive – over five million articles culled from 3,000 publications
- company briefs
- market prices
- country briefs
- industry briefs
- portfolio
- life.

This truly is a resource for the seriously committed and dedicated investor. However, try this site: **www.ftquicken.co.uk.**

As you will see, this is also the *Financial Times*. However, this time they share the sponsorship of it with Quicken, the software product for keeping track of your finances. This site is devoted to personal finances generally, and it has sections on:

- investments
- insurance
- mortgages
- tax centre
- savings and loans
- pensions
- currency markets.

Each section has articles from the *Financial Times* contributors, in a rather more accessible style than the main *Financial Times* site.

Wall Street Journal Interactive Edition   www.wsj.com

Our cousins across the pond would probably dispute the supremacy of the *Financial Times*. This is their contender for the title. This is certainly the USA's premier financial newspaper, and if your investment interests are slanted towards America, this is the one to read.

The Economist   www.economist.com

This is another heavyweight. It describes itself as 'The International Journal of News, Ideas, Opinion and Analysis'. Besides financial matters, it covers more general news and current affairs, and it is a rather more literary magazine than other financial journals. Its sections cover:

- book reviews
- weekly economic indicators
- infrequently asked questions (devious puzzles about world affairs – with answers)
- the best of *The Economist* – past articles
- the two most recent back issues of the journal
- online bookshop
- top jobs
- the style guide – a guide to good English, used by all writers for *The Economist*.

You cannot access the full magazine without paying the normal subscription. However, this site does give a good flavour of what the magazine is like. This is a magazine for the serious reader – and one who is literate as well as numerate.

Financial Mail online	www.thisismoney.co.uk

This is the financial section of the *Daily Mail*, the *Mail on Sunday*, and the *Evening Standard*. In its online form it goes by the name of 'This is Money – your personal finance adviser'. The home page has a selection of headlines and articles such as appear in the money section of the newspapers. There are also more specialised parts of the site, including:

- news and markets
- saving and investing
- mortgages and homes
- pensions
- insurance
- taxes
- small business
- how to spend it
- ask the experts
- fact files.

There is also a daily updated 'Moneywatch' section with the latest index figures for the major world share indexes. You can also set up your own portfolio details which will be updated at the same time, showing the comparison with the major indexes. You can get individual company prices in a search facility.

Another section of the site advises you on 'Money savers'. This points you to the best deals on mortgage rates, personal loans, credit card deals, life insurance and overdrafts. The 'Money makers' section gives information about unit trusts, top savings rates, investment trusts, ISAs, Internet banking and online share dealing.

This is a good overall site, with many practical features. The 'Fact Files' are particularly useful – specially written guides on a whole host of topics.

The Times www.times-money.co.uk

The money section of *The Times*, and in particular its weekend money section, are included in this online magazine.

The Electronic Telegraph www.telegraph.co.uk

This gives the City and Finance section of the *Daily Telegraph*.

Investors Chronicle www.investorschronicle.co.uk

This is the online version of the renowned journal, giving top class advice on a whole range of finance-related subjects. This publication is aimed at the serious investor. A certain degree of investment sophistication is implied – although there is a beginners section. The aim is that a beginner will quickly get 'up to speed'. The web site requires you to register, but this is free. Once registered, you can browse the current issue of the magazine, and access the other parts of the web site. These include:

- Questions and answers – on commonly raised questions, grouped under personal finance, shares or tax.
- Absolute beginners – articles from past issues are collected here to guide beginners into the finer points of investing.
- Bookshop – a well-stocked bookshop, of specialist titles. Delivery is promised within two or three days.
- IC innovations – not just a magazine. This is really just a shop window for their own products – mainly books. There is also an 'investment ledger' offered for sale, to help you keep track of your investments and their performance.
- Back issues – selected articles from past issues.
- Annual reports – details of the annual reports of companies, of interest to investors.

In addition to these are e-zines – magazines or journals published only on the Internet.

Bull and Bear www.bullandbear.com

This is the cyber pub, where investors can meet friends and discuss information and opinions about financial matters – with or without a pint in their hand. As well as information on shares, and futures trading, there is a chat forum, and there will soon be courses where serious students can learn about financial matters.

Excite	www.excite.co.uk

This site is a search engine which thinks it is an e-zine. It has several channels of information, one of which is 'Money and Investing'. The main sections are:

- insurance
- investment
- mortgages
- pensions
- savings and banking
- tax.

There are various tools – such as a currency converter and a mortgage calculator, best investments, top savings rates, and insurance quotes. The FTSE 100 and Dow Jones indexes are updated (20 minutes delay from real time). There are updated prices for most shares (again with a 20-minute delay from real time).

Financial Information Net Directory	www.find.co.uk

This site offers links to many other sites. It is owned by Omnium Communications Ltd. The home page gives you options for several aspects of financial information. The pages are populated by the lenders who use this site to set out their stall, and there are many banner advertisements. This is a good jumping-off point to search for information and companies in practically any financial field (see Figure 13).

FT Your Money	www.ftyourmoney.com

This is another site run by the *Financial Times*. As you would expect with such credentials, it is an excellent site, with much wisdom and information. Any advice given is carefully targeted towards people in particular circumstances. For instance, it gives a recommended division of your savings money into different types of savings. The advice differs for:

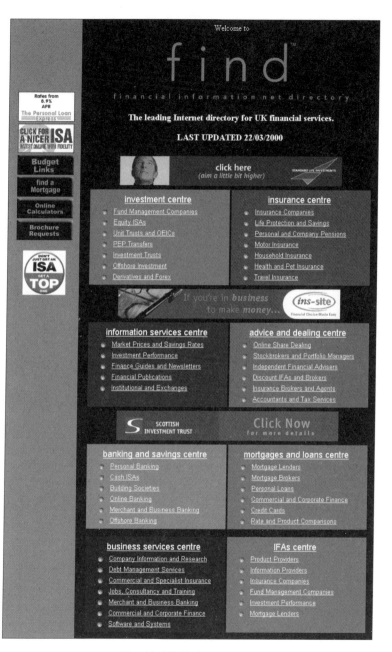

Fig. 13. FIND home page.

- young and single
- young and married/attached – no children
- young and married/attached – with children
- middle aged, with children approaching further education
- pre-retirement.

The main sections of the site are:

- your life
    - home buying
    - living together
    - retirement
    - education
- your opportunities
    - saving money
    - creating wealth
- finding an adviser
- getting organised
- tax saving
- your decisions
    - mortgages
    - insurance
    - savings and credit
    - investments
    - pensions.

There is also a news room, regularly updated. This is a site well worth visiting. It should have something of help for everybody.

Interactive Investor International   www.iii.co.uk

To quote: 'The ultimate goal of interactive investor is to provide you with all the information you need to make an investment decision.' The site aims to provide the best information possible to help investors make their decisions. Naturally, this includes some advertising banners on the site, but there are also many independent sources, such as Micropal, FT Extel, and so on, to give you in-depth investment information online. The site includes:

- discussion forums on individual UK equities
- advice on several levels (e.g. 'Ask an expert', 'find an IFA', personal finance guides, etc.)
- 'centres' for various topics such as mortgages, savings, insurance, new issues, banking, etc.
- performance statistics for shares, unit trusts, pensions, etc.
- portfolio tools
- news (with late-breaking news featured)
- quotes for share prices
- a directory of product providers.

Money Advisor   www.moneyadvisor.com

This is an American site, so the content is biased towards the USA, but it does have some useful tools, and its stated goal is to provide tools for consumers to make decisions about their finances.

Money Shop   www.moneyshop.co.uk

This is a site, like Financial Information Net Directory, which mainly provides links to financial web sites. The categories are:

- banking and saving
- investment
- financial advice
- general insurance
- mortgages and loans
- life insurance
- pensions
- other links

Besides the links, there are 'insider guides' to the various categories, which provide useful information.

Moneyweb   www.moneyweb.co.uk

This is a site maintained by Ian Dickson, who describes himself as 'a financial services insider for many years, but who is now free to tell it as it is'. His site has 'solid information for the layman; speculations and fun for the professional'. His proud boast (from an article in the

Financial Times) is that it is 'probably the most comprehensive UK personal finance site'.

His navigation page is in the form of an index, so you look for what you want in alphabetical order. There is a wealth of in-depth articles on many subjects, with an emphasis on not getting ripped off.

Moneywise   www.moneywise.co.uk

This is the financial magazine of *Readers Digest*. It is backed by their enormous resources, and has all the features you would expect – plus, inevitably for *Readers Digest*, a prize draw.

MoneyWorld   www.moneyworld.co.uk

This is a commercial company, so it is dependent on advertisements. However, it has sections on home buying, insurance, savings, stock market, tax, currencies, online banking and online trading, funds appraisal for unit trusts, investment trusts, pension and life funds.

Motley Fool   www.fool.co.uk

This is one of the most highly regarded online financial e-zines, in both its British and its American incarnations (you can access the American version at: www.fool.com).

The Motley Fool has a quirky style all of its own, but don't ignore it because of that. It was started in 1993 by two American brothers. The name derives from British history, when the court jester (The Fool) was the privileged person who could tell the monarch the truth, without getting his head chopped off!

The 'mission statement' of the Motley Fool is to demystify investment and finance matters so that ordinary people can understand the principles involved. This is reinforced by their four basic principles (see Figure 14):

1. You are the most capable person alive to manage your money.

2. This stuff isn't rocket science; we all just need to learn together.

3. Being smart about your money can be a lot of fun – really!

4. You can make a fortune doing it.

The web site is attractive and easy to navigate. Registration is easy, and if you don't like the weird password they give you, you can change

Welcome to the Fool

What is the Motley Fool? Founded in the USA in 1993 by brothers David and Tom Gardner, the Foolish message has been successfully transported across the Atlantic to the UK. Our name derives from Elizabethan drama, where only the court jester (the "Fool") could tell the King the truth without getting his head lopped off. In the UK for since 1987, we've been dedicated to educating, amusing and enriching individuals in search of the truth.

"Those who understand compound interest are destined to collect it. Those who don't are doomed to pay it."

What is the truth? The stark truth is that the financial world preys on ignorance and fear. Few schools teach personal finance and investing. As a result, most folks grow up afraid to admit that they don't understand how to do things like invest in the stock market, buy a house, buy a car or handle their credit cards responsibly. True, none of these topics are great mysteries, but without a proper education, all of them can be intimidating and confusing.

But now you've set your virtual feet on Foolish soil, and your days of fear and intimidation are over. We exist to serve you, to teach you -- and to have a heck of a lot of fun along the way. We believe that:

1. You are the most capable person alive to manage your money.
2. This stuff isn't rocket science; we all just need to learn together.
3. Being smart about your money can be a lot of fun... really!
4. You can make a fortune doing it.

So now it's time for your first Foolish experience. You can take the full site tour or do the quick version. Or, you can just click on the links below to be instantly transported to some of the most popular areas of the site.

Learn how to save and invest in 10 easy steps.
Plan for a happy and fruitful retirement.
The Fool's Guide to ISAs
Understand Pensions (yes, it IS possible)
Learn about & discuss technology stocks

Take a tour | The once-over (a really quick tour) | Free registration

Messages | News | Stock Ideas | Portfolios | Finance | Fool's School

Fig. 14. Motley Fool's four beliefs.

it. Within seconds of registering, you get a message on your email, telling you all about the Motley Fool, and how to get the best out of it. This site welcomes beginners, and there is a 'Fool's School'. There are also several message boards, where you can join the chat.

This is a star site, and those who join are quickly addicted to it.

Reuters   www.reuters.com

This is the famous news agency. Their boast is that they are the world's leading financial information and news group. It is, of course, an American company, but it is the world leader in gathering financial news from around the world.

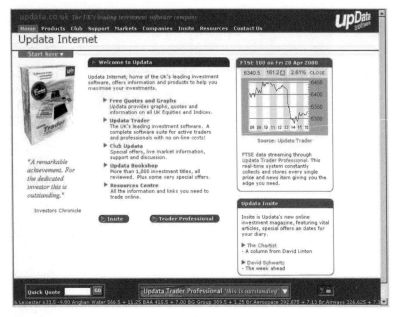

Fig. 15. Updata home page.

Tipsheets.co.uk   www.tipsheets.co.uk

This is a site which gives you access to all the UK investment newsletters issued by firms regulated by the Personal Investment Authority. The site also has a bookshop, latest news, investment magazines, links, and telephone share prices.

UK-iNvest   www.uk-invest.com

This site is operated by GlobalNetFinancial. It is mainly concerned with stock market investing, although it does also have sections on other areas such as personal finance, and links to Mrs Cohen's diary and The Motley Fool. It encourages readers to register – for free – to get free email alerts on financial news, special interviews with financial gurus, other 'special events', portfolio and investment tools, and discounts on books.

Updata   www.updata.co.uk

This site provides investment software and up-to-date information to help you invest. Well worth a visit if you are serious about stock market investment. (See Figure 15.)

Yahoo! Finance   http://finance.uk.yahoo.com

This started out not as a magazine but as a search engine dedicated to financial sites. However, the site does now have editorials, finance news, personal finance, quotes on prices of shares and indexes, articles, message boards and chat – in fact, all you would expect from an Internet magazine.

14

Summary of Web Sites

In this book, we have looked at many web sites. On the following pages is a concise summary of most of the sites, and the subjects they cover.

Name	Web site	Loans and mortgages	Banking	Internet service	Home and contents insurance	Pet insurance	Wedding insurance	Personal accident insurance	Legal insurance	Business insurance	Motor insurance	Travel insurance	Medical/health insurance	Saving and investing	Pensions	Life assurance	Share dealing and derivatives	Professional advisers	Traded endowment policies	Investing information/advice	Magazines/journals/papers	Regulators/watchdogs
Bull and Bear	www.bullandbear.com																			✗		
BUPA	www.bupa.co.uk												✗									
Car Insurance Centre	www.carsource.co.uk										✗	✗										
CGU Insurance	www.cgu-direct.co.uk				✗						✗	✗				✗						
Charles Schwab	www.schwab-worldwide.com																✗					
Cheltenham & Gloucester	www.cheltglos.co.uk	✗																				
Chesham BS	www.cheshambsoc.co.uk	✗												✗								
Churchill	www.churchill.co.uk	✗			✗						✗	✗										
CIS Pensions	www.cis.co.uk													✗	✗	✗						
Citibank	www.citibank.com		✗	✗																		
Clerical Medical Investment Group	www.clericalmedical.co.uk													✗	✗	✗						
Club Direct	www.clubdirect.co.uk											✗										
CMC	www.forex-cmc.com																✗					
Columbus Direct	www.columbusdirect.co.uk											✗										
Co-operative Bank	https://co-operativebank.co.uk	✗	✗																			
Co-operative Insurance Services	www.cis.co.uk																					
Cornhill	www.cornhill.co.uk				✗					✗	✗	✗		✗	✗	✗						
Coutts & Co.	www.coutts.com		✗		✗	✗	✗				✗					✗						
C S Healthcare	www.cshealthcare.co.uk												✗									
DAS	www.das.co.uk								✗													
Day Trading Stocks	www.daytradingstocks.com																			✗		
Department for Social Security	www.dss.gov.uk													✗	✗							

Name	Web site	Loans and mortgages	Banking	Internet service	Home and contents insurance	Pet insurance	Wedding insurance	Personal accident insurance	Legal insurance	Business insurance	Motor insurance	Travel insurance	Medical/health insurance	Saving and investing	Pensions	Life assurance	Share dealing and derivatives	Professional advisers	Traded endowment policies	Investing information/advice	Magazines/journals/papers	Regulators/watchdogs
Direct Line	www.directline.com	X			X	X					X	X		X	X	X						
Discount Pensions	www.discountpensions.co.uk														X							
DLJ Direct	www.dljdirect.co.uk																X					
Downunder Insurance	www.downunderinsurance.co.uk									X	X	X										
Eagle Star	www.eaglestardirect.co.uk									X	X	X		X								
Ecclesiastical Insurance Group	www.eigonline.co.uk										X	X										
Eclipse Insurance	www.eclipse-insurance.co.uk				X		X															
Economist	www.economist.com																				X	
E Cortal	www.e-cortal.co.uk													X			X					
Egg	www.egg.com	X	X		X							X										
Elite Mortgages Ltd.	www.elitemortgages.co.uk	X																				
Equitable Life	www.equitable.co.uk									X				X	X	X						
Etax Ltd.	www.etax.co.uk																	X				
E*Trade	www.etrade.co.uk																X			X		
Excite	www.excite.com																				X	
Exeter Friendly Society	www.exeterfriendly.co.uk												X									
Exeter Fund Managers	www.chameleon-isa.co.uk													X								
Fastrade	www.fastrade.co.uk													X			X					
Fidelity	www.fidelity.co.uk													X								
Financial Mail Online	www.thisismoney.co.uk																				X	
Financial Services Authority	www.sib.co.uk																					X
Financial Times	www.ft.com																				X	

Name	Web site	Loans and mortgages	Banking	Internet service	Home and contents insurance	Pet insurance	Wedding insurance	Personal accident insurance	Legal insurance	Business insurance	Motor insurance	Travel insurance	Medical/health insurance	Saving and investing	Pensions	Life assurance	Share dealing and derivatives	Professional advisers	Traded endowment policies	Investing information/advice	Magazines/journals/papers	Regulators/watchdogs
Firebond Insurance	www.firebond.co.uk										✗					✗						
First Direct	www.firstdirect.co.uk	✗	✗																			
First-e	www.first-e.com		✗																			
First Global Insurances	www.ins-site.co.uk																					
First National Motor Finance	www.firstnationalmotorfinance.co.uk	✗																				
First People's Mortgage	www.first.co.uk										✗											
First Trust Bank	www.ftbni.co.uk		✗																			
Fleming	www.flemings.co.uk																					
Foreign and Colonial	www.fandc.co.uk													✗	✗							
Framlington	www.framlington.co.uk													✗								
Friend Indeed Friendly Society	www.friend-indeed.co.uk													✗								
Friends Provident	www.friendsprovident.co.uk							✗														
Gartmore	www.gartmore.co.uk													✗								
Gladiator Insurance Services	www.gladiator.co.uk										✗											
Halifax	www.halifax.co.uk	✗	✗								✗	✗		✗	✗	✗						
Healthy Pets	www.healthy-pets.co.uk					✗																
Henderson Investors	www.henderson.com													✗								
Hill Samuel	www.isa-2000.co.uk													✗								
Hospital Savings Association	www.hsahealthcare.org												✗									
HSBC	www.hsbc.co.uk	✗	✗		✗					✗												
IFA Promotion Ltd.	www.unbiased.co.uk																					✗
Independent Financial Advisers Association	www.ifaa.org.uk																					✗

Name	Web site	Loans and mortgages	Banking	Internet service	Home and contents insurance	Pet insurance	Wedding insurance	Personal accident insurance	Legal insurance	Business insurance	Motor insurance	Travel insurance	Medical/health insurance	Saving and investing	Pensions	Life assurance	Share dealing and derivatives	Professional advisers	Traded endowment policies	Investing information/advice	Magazines/journals/papers	Regulators/watchdogs
Instant Mortgage Centre	www.loans4u.co.uk	✗																				
Institute of Financial Planning	www.financialplanning.org.uk																					✗
Insurance Line	www.insurance-line.co.uk				✗						✗											
Insurance Policy Trading Co.	www.endowments-direct.co.uk																		✗			
Insurance Ombudsman	www.thejob.org.uk																					✗
Interactive Investor International	www.iii.co.uk																				✗	
Internet Fraud Watch	www.fraud.org																					✗
Internet Scam Busters	www.scambusters.com																					✗
Intersure	www.intersure.co.uk				✗		✗				✗	✗										
Investors Chronicle	www.investorschronicle.co.uk													✗							✗	
Jupiter	www.jupiteronline.co.uk													✗		✗						
Lambeth BS	www.simplydirect.co.uk	✗			✗							✗		✗								
Leeds and Holbeck BS	www.leeds-holbeck.co.uk	✗								✗	✗		✗	✗		✗						
Legal & General	www.landg.com	✗			✗									✗	✗							
Liverpool Victoria	www.lvbestbonds.co.uk	✗			✗					✗			✗	✗	✗							
Lloyds TSB Bank	www.lloydstsb.co.uk	✗	✗		✗									✗	✗							
M and G	www.mandg.co.uk		✗											✗	✗	✗						
Marks and Spencer	www.marks-and-spencer.co.uk	✗												✗								
Medibroker	www.medibroker.com												✗									
Medicus	www.medicus.co.uk												✗									
Mercury Asset Management	www.mam.com													✗								
MGM Assurance	www.mgm-assurance.co.uk															✗						

Name	Web site	Loans and mortgages	Banking	Internet service	Home and contents insurance	Pet insurance	Wedding insurance	Personal accident insurance	Legal insurance	Business insurance	Motor insurance	Travel insurance	Medical/health insurance	Saving and investing	Pensions	Life assurance	Share dealing and derivatives	Professional advisers	Traded endowment policies	Investing information/advice	Magazines/journals/papers	Regulators/watchdogs
Money Advisor	www.moneyadvisor.com	×												×						×		
Moneynet	www.moneynet.co.uk																				×	
Money Shop	www.moneyshop.co.uk																				×	
Moneyweb	www.moneyweb.co.uk																			×		
Moneywise	www.moneywise.co.uk																				×	
Moneyworld	www.moneyworld.co.uk																				×	
Mortgages Online	www.mortgates-online.co.uk	×																				
Motley Fool	www.fool.co.uk																			×	×	×
Nasdaq Market	www.nasdaq.com																×					
National Mutual	www.nationalmutual.co.uk				×										×		×					
National Savings	www.nationalsavings.co.uk													×								
Nationwide BS	www.nationwide.co.uk	×	×	×										×								
NatWest Bank	www.natwest.co.uk	×	×											×			×					
Newcastle BS	www.newcastle.co.uk	×												×								
Newton Fund Managers	www.newton.co.uk										×			×	×	×	×					
NFU Mutual	www.nfumutual.co.uk				×	×				×	×	×			×	×						
Nomad Travel Insurance	www.nomad-insurance.co.uk											×										
Norwich Union	www.norwich-union.co.uk				×					×	×		×	×		×						
Office of Fair Trading	www.oft.gov.uk																					×
Offshore Alert	www.offshorebusiness.com																					×
Online Life Assurance Service	www.financial-guidance-centre.co.uk															×						
Options Direct (Europe) Ltd	www.options-direct.co.uk																×					

Name	Web site	Loans and mortgages	Banking	Internet service	Home and contents insurance	Pet insurance	Wedding insurance	Personal accident insurance	Legal insurance	Business insurance	Motor insurance	Travel insurance	Medical/health insurance	Saving and investing	Pensions	Life assurance	Share dealing and derivatives	Professional advisers	Traded endowment policies	Investing information/advice	Magazines/journals/papers	Regulators/watchdogs
Perpetual Investment Management	www.perpetual.co.uk													✗								
Pet Healthcare Insurance	www.pethealthcare.co.uk					✗																
Pet Plan	www.petplan.co.uk					✗																
Petshield	www.petproducts.co.uk					✗																
PHA Travel Insurance	www.demon.co.uk/dayco											✗										
Plain English Campaign	www.plainenglish.co.uk																					✗
PolicyPlus	www.policyplus.com															✗						
Preferential Direct	www.preferential.co.uk											✗										
Prime Health	www.primehealth.co.uk											✗	✗									
Private Health Associates	www.phahealth.co.uk											✗	✗									
Private Health Partnership	www.php.co.uk											✗	✗									
Private Patients Plan	www.ppphealthcare.co.uk												✗									
Prudential	www.pru.co.uk	✗			✗					✗	✗		✗	✗	✗	✗						
Reuters	www.reuters.com									✗										✗		
Riley's Insurance	http://freespace.virgin.net/rileys.insurance				✗						✗	✗										
Royal and Sun Alliance	www.rsa-investments.co.uk				✗					✗	✗	✗	✗	✗								
Royal Bank of Scotland	www.royalbankscot.co.uk	✗	✗																			
Royal Liver Assurance	www.royal-liver.com				✗								✗	✗	✗							
Royal London Insurance	www.royal-london.ins.co.uk	✗									✗			✗	✗	✗						
RT2 Trader	www.rt2trader.co.uk																✗					
Saga	www.saga.co.uk				✗						✗	✗	✗	✗								
Schroders	www.schroder.co.uk													✗								

Name	Web site	Loans and mortgages	Banking	Internet service	Home and contents insurance	Pet insurance	Wedding insurance	Personal accident insurance	Legal insurance	Business insurance	Motor insurance	Travel insurance	Medical/health insurance	Saving and investing	Pensions	Life assurance	Share dealing and derivatives	Professional advisers	Traded endowment policies	Investing information/advice	Magazines/journals/papers	Regulators/watchdogs
Scottish Friendly Society	www.scottishfriendly.co.uk													×		×						
Scottish Pet Insurance	www.scotpet.co.uk					×																
Scottish Widows	www.scottishwidows.co.uk	×												×	×	×						
Screentrade	www.screentrade.com				×						×	×				×						
Skandia	www.skandia.co.uk													×		×						
Standard and Poors	www.standardandpoors.com																			×		
Standard Chartered Bank	www.stanchart.com		×																			
Standard Life	www.standardlife.co.uk														×	×						
Standard Life Bank	www.standardlifebank.com	×	×											×								
Stock Detective	www.stockdetective.com												×				×					×
Stocktrade	www.stocktrade.co.uk													×	×	×						
Stockwiz	www.stockwiz.com											×		×	×	×				×		
Sun Life	www.axaequityandlaw.co.uk													×	×							
Sun Life of Canada	www.slocpensions.co.uk	×				×								×	×	×						
Surrenda-link Ltd.	www.surrendalink.u-net.com																			×		
Teachers BS	www.teachersbs.co.uk	×			×						×			×								
Teachers Group	www.teachers-group.co.uk	×	×	×	×						×			×								
Tesco	www.tesco.co.uk	×												×								
The Biz	www.thebiz.co.uk					×							×	×	×							
The Mortgage Guild	www.theguild.co.uk	×											×	×								
The Research Department	www.trd.co.uk																			×	×	
The Telegraph	www.telegraph.co.uk																				×	

Name	Web site	Loans and mortgages	Banking	Internet service	Home and contents insurance	Pet insurance	Wedding insurance	Personal accident insurance	Legal insurance	Business insurance	Motor insurance	Travel insurance	Medical/health insurance	Saving and investing	Pensions	Life assurance	Share dealing and derivatives	Professional advisers	Traded endowment policies	Investing information/advice	Magazines/journals/papers	Regulators/watchdogs
The Times	www.times-money.co.uk																				x	
The Travel Insurance Club	www.travelinsuranceclub.co.uk											x										
Threadneedle Investments	www.threadneedle.co.uk													x						x		
Tipsheets	www.tipsheets.co.uk																				x	
Triodos Bank	www.triodos.co.uk		x											x								
Tunstall Insurance Society	www.tunstallassurance.co.uk													x		x						
UK-Invest	www.uk-invest.co.uk													x								
UK Mortgage Brokers	www.mortgagebroker.co.uk	x																				
Under the Sun Travel Insurance	www.underthesun.co.uk											x										
Virgin Direct	www.virgin-direct.co.uk	x	x											x	x	x						
Wall Street Journal	http://public.wsj.com																				x	
Western Provident Association	www.wpahealth.co.uk												x									
William Russell International	www.william-russell.co.uk	x											x									
Woolwich plc	www.woolwich.co.uk	x																				
World Cover Direct	www.worldcover.com											x										
Worldtrekker	www.worldtrekker.com											x										
Worldwide Travel Insurance	www.wtis.co.uk											x										
Xest	www.xest.com																x					
Yahoo! Finance	http://finance.uk.yahoo.com																			x	x	
Yellow Brick Road	www.yellowbrickroad.co.uk	x																				

Glossary

Address A string of letters or numbers to type into your computer to find a web site or an email.

Broker An intermediary between the consumer and the provider, e.g. for insurances, or dealing on the Stock Exchange.

Collective investment An investment which takes relatively small amounts of money from many investors into a common pool and invests in a large number of companies, thus spreading the risk.

Convertibles A type of preference share in a company, giving the right to convert those shares into ordinary shares.

Corporate bonds A form of loan to a company.

Customs and Excise The government body responsible for collecting customs and excise duty and VAT.

Day trading A form of speculation involving buying and selling shares on the same day in the hope of making a profit.

Derivatives A way of speculating on the prices of shares.

Dividend The reward, or sharing in profit, paid to ordinary shareholders in a company.

Email A way of communicating with another computer through the Internet.

Encryption A method of encoding information sent over the Internet so that it can only be read by the intended recipient.

Endowment policy A type of life assurance policy combining the protection of life cover with a savings element.

Endowment mortgage A method of repaying a mortgage by paying premiums to an endowment policy and using the proceeds to repay the mortgage.

Equities Ordinary shares in a company, giving a participation in profits – the dividend.

E-zine A magazine published only on the Internet.

Flexible mortgage A hybrid of a bank account and a mortgage loan.

Friendly Society A type of organisation which can offer tax-exempt savings products.

FTSE 100 An index of the composite prices of the top 100 shares traded on the London Stock Exchange.

Home income plan A way of realising some of the value locked up in your house.

Impaired credit A record at credit agencies showing that you have had a default in paying a debt.

Income multiplier A measure used by mortgage lenders to ensure you can keep up repayments on a mortgage.

Inland Revenue The government body responsible for collecting taxes.

Investment trust A type of collective investment.

ISA An investment with tax advantages.

ISP Internet Service Provider. A company which provides you with a connection to the Internet.

Loan to valuation A measure used by mortgage lenders to determine how much they can lend on a certain property.

Microsoft Money Computer program to help you organise your finances.

Modem Device to connect your computer to the Internet.

Mortgage A loan secured on a property.

Mortgage indemnity guarantee An insurance taken out against the possibility of not being able to repay your mortgage loan.

Mortgage protection insurance Life assurance policy taken out to ensure that a mortgage is repaid if you should die.

National Savings A government organisation offering many types of savings products, some with tax advantages.

Negative equity The situation which occurs when the value of your house is less than the amount you owe on your mortgage.

OEIC Open ended investment company – a type of collective investment.

Options A way of speculating on the prices of shares.

Pension mortgage A method of repaying a mortgage by paying premiums to a pension policy and using the lump sum option on maturity to repay the mortgage.

Preference shares A class of shares in a company which give a fixed rate of interest rather than variable dividends, but have a preference over ordinary shares in the event of liquidation.

Quicken Computer program to help you organise your finances.

Search engine A device to find web sites relating to a subject or containing a word or words.

Stock exchange An organised and regulated market for buying and selling shares.

Traded endowment policies A market which has grown up for people wishing to cash in endowment policies early to sell them to people who wish to use them as an investment.

Unit trust A type of collective investment.

Further Reading

Books

Saving and Investing, John Whiteley, How To Books.

Managing Your Personal Finances, John Claxton, How To Books.

Investing in Stocks and Shares, Dr John White, How To Books.

Investment Made Easy, Jim Slater, Orion Books.

The Zulu Principle, Jim Slater, Orion Books.

The Online Investor, Peter Temple, John Wiley.

Securing a Rewarding Retirement, Norman Toulson, How To Books.

Dealing With Your Bank, Brian Cain, How To Books.

Money Saving Mortgages, Tony Cornell, How To Books.

Arranging Insurance, Terry Hallett, How To Books.

Coping with Self Assessment, John Whiteley, How To Books.

Paying Less Tax, John Whiteley, How To Books.

Getting Started in Shares, Peter Temple, John Wiley.

Using the Internet, Graham Jones, How To Books.

Success With the Internet, Allen Wyatt, Jamsa Press.

The Internet Unleashed, Steven Bang, SAMS Publishing.

The Internet – The Rough Guide, Angus J Kennedy, Rough Guides.

MAGAZINE

Internet Investor, Future Publishing.

Index